Let
your past
GO and
LIVE

Avril Carruthers

Let your past GO and LIVE

Freedom from
family, relationship
and work baggage

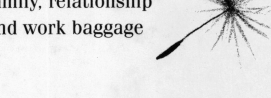

inspired
LIVING

ALLEN&UNWIN

First published in 2008

Inspired Living, an imprint of
Allen & Unwin
83 Alexander Street
Crows Nest NSW 2065
Australia
Phone: (61 2) 8425 0100
Fax: (61 2) 9906 2218
Email: info@allenandunwin.com
Web: www.allenandunwin.com

National Library of Australia
Cataloguing-in-Publication entry:

Carruthers, Avril.

Let your past go and live : freedom from family,
   relationship and work baggage / Avril Carruthers.

ISBN: 9781741755206 (pbk.)

Includes index.
Bibliography.

Self-actualization (Psychology)
Self-realization.
Self-acceptance.
Interpersonal relations.

158.1

Internal design by fisheye design
Set in 10.5/14 pt Minion by Midland Typesetters, Australia
Printed and bound in Australia by Griffin Press

10 9 8 7 6 5 4 3

Mixed Sources
Product group from well-managed forests, and other controlled sources
www.fsc.org Cert no. SGS-COC-005088
© 1996 Forest Stewardship Council

The paper in this book is FSC certified. FSC promotes environmentally responsible, socially beneficial and economically viable management of the world's forests.

Contents

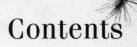

Acknowledgments

My profound thanks for all I have received from my teachers, some of whom I've known in the flesh and others whom I have only known through their writings and correspondence.

Dr Samuel Sagan, and the good people of the Clairvision School, Sydney; Dr David Schnarch; Dr Eric Berne; Dr Thomas Harris; Dr Stephen B. Karpman; Elana Leigh; Jan Grant; Eric Lyleson; Lao-Tzu.

Dianne Blayney, Posie Graeme-Evans, Isolde Martyn, Peter O'Donnell and Nicola Tomlin, all of whom helped in so many ways with feedback and suggestions.

Maggie Hamilton at Allen & Unwin for her constant encouragement and advice; my brilliant editor and copyeditor Clara Finlay and Katri Hilden; Clare Emery for proofreading; and Kathy Mossop who made everything so much easier.

My extraordinary clients, students and supervisees and all those who attended my workshops, always my teachers.

To my ever-supportive family, my undying appreciation.

Self is everywhere, shining forth from all beings,
vaster than the vast, subtler than the most subtle,
unreachable, yet nearer than breath, than heartbeat.
Eye cannot see it, ear cannot hear it nor tongue
utter it; only in deep absorption can the mind,
grown pure and silent, merge with the formless truth.
As soon as you find it, you are free; you have found yourself;
you have solved the great riddle; your heart forever is at peace.
Whole, you enter the Whole. Your personal self
returns to its radiant, intimate, deathless source.

Mundaka Upanishad
(c. 8th–5th century BCE)

Introduction

If our past shapes us, is it permanent? Can we ever become free of it?

Few of us are not limited in some way by events in our past, and while our parents are frequently (and often unfairly) blamed for our deficiencies, none of us is perfect and it is not only our parents who have determined who we are.

There are parts of our lives with which we might be less than satisfied. We might wish we were more effective or successful or that our relationships were more fulfilling. But often it is not just a matter of being more effective or more successful in our lives, or about being loved or loving in the way we wish. Often it is a feeling that we are not in control of our lives, or not expressing ourselves as we truly are. We find ourselves acting in ways that we would rather not. We may feel the 'real' us hasn't yet come out, or that parts of us are frozen or undeveloped. Or perhaps we really don't know who we are and we hope we are not who we seem to be, or who people seem to think we are.

To find out who we are, it's easier to start with who we are not. In working out how we can become more 'authentic' it helps to have a structured approach. As a transpersonal psychotherapist I work with people who want not only to find effective approaches to personal problems, but also to explore possibilities, to grow as human beings to where life is exciting, challenging and fun. At a certain stage there is a spiritual element that goes beyond the physical and material to a sense of something far greater than ourselves.

We have the ability to connect to this greater something in our daily interactions. I work holistically, as an energetic healer where needed, as well as in more conventional modes of talk therapy. I use subtle vision and facilitate in clients altered states of awareness that can reveal the source of a problem and defuse it, enabling lasting change. Often sessions are deeply meditative in nature. The aim is to connect people to more meaningful experiences of themselves, to increase spiritual consciousness and personal freedom. As a result this book deals with deep states of awareness as well as Aha! moments that can liberate us from identifying with our limitations. This book represents the major part of my work with clients and students specifically on Characters.

Characters are sub-personalities that are conditioned into us and which we hide behind—and which often take over at the most inappropriate times. Characters show us different aspects—fragmented reflections—of ourselves, like a mosaic made of fragments of mirror. One aim of working with Characters is that eventually we see ourselves truly, no longer fractured or distorted, but whole and a pleasure to see. Working with Characters is life-changing.

Many of the explorations in this book come directly from workshops and sessions with clients, or from my own life and observations. Those clients whose stories are partly reproduced here have graciously agreed to their inclusion. I am grateful for their generosity and honesty, and for sharing their explorations in the service of a better understanding of Characters. I hope you will find the Character capsules and commentaries as fascinating as we have, and that you are able to make this approach to self-realisation useful.

In this book I have used a capital letter to differentiate what I mean by Character, from *character* in the more usual sense as a person's distinguishing qualities or moral constitution. I also commonly refer to a Character's emotion with a capital letter to differentiate it from a more transient emotion. So, an Angry Character is different to a person who may occasionally get angry at something, but is not chronically angry at everything in his life. A Sad or Grief-struck Character is sad about everything, not just an event or situation that warrants it on occasion. When talking about Professional Characters, I am referring to a set of formulaic behaviours adopted by some people in the pursuit of their professions: for example, the Doctor Character, Accountant or Teacher. And to avoid the clumsiness of 'he or she' I have alternated between using both genders.

The many stories in these pages are not intended to be clinical case studies, but rather capsules designed to exemplify points for Character differentiation or identification. While each Character is based on a number of different people, none is intended to identify a specific, living person; rather I have sought to depict a Character in its most typical form, and aimed for emotional truth rather than biographical facts. It is not intended that Characters are identified with either gender where a Character is not gender-specific. In general, a Character is not the whole person. It is a construct and not quite authentic.

Similarly, I also refer to a conscious and deliberate Role with a capital letter to differentiate it from a role in the ordinary sense. A Character can consciously be 'taken over' and made into a Role—a more evolved and higher functioning way of behaving and relating, where we are no longer enslaved by the unconscious compulsions and limitations of our Characters, and where we become more authentic and true. The calm rationality of a Role is like a peaceful island in a sea of sharks. Through this process we can eventually come to our Archetype—the individual blueprint or higher design that we may sense is guiding our evolution, and the limitless potential within us that is waiting to unfold.

In essence, this book is about a spiritual quest. It's about finding out who we truly are and our place in the universe. It's about finding a path that leads us to the divine spark within us, that takes us home to oneness.

I hope this books helps you on your own personal journey towards healing and wholeness.

Avril Carruthers

PART I

A cast of thousands:
Characters

All the world's a stage,

And all the men and women merely players:

They have their exits and their entrances;

And one man in his time plays many parts.

William Shakespeare

As You Like It (Act 2, scene 7)

1

Slipping out of Character

Tara and Sean met while skiing and in the fire of their instant mutual attraction wondered why the entire mountain had not immediately melted. It became a joke between them—that somehow they seemed to be existing on an exalted, parallel universe.

Being in love, the world shone with extraordinary magic. Their breath stopped for long moments in the silence of pristine fallen snow. Sunlit ice hanging from trees sparked sudden tears of joy. In the exhilaration of flying down the mountain on skis they felt like gods. At the end of each perfect day their heads touched over mugs of mulled glühwein around the open fireplace where they read complete acceptance in each other's eyes. Shared laughter deepened a delicious sense of expansion and infinite possibility. Each felt they had met The One. By the end of their holiday—two short weeks—they had decided to live together. Within a month of moving in, they decided to get married. Such was the momentum of their holiday romance—but so much is ignored when we are in love that it wasn't until the wedding night that serious alarm bells began to ring for Tara. By the end of their honeymoon Tara was inwardly disillusioned, bewildered and disappointed.

And once they were back home in the city, going to work, Tara and Sean found to their increasing dismay that the person they thought to be their soulmate was someone else. Their love was not enough. In reality, their values, backgrounds and intellectual interests were poles apart—even though they had seemed in perfect agreement on holiday. Their styles of communicating were also incompatible. Sean rarely talked about his feelings and was oblivious to his own or other people's emotions. On the other hand, Tara was acutely aware of how she and others were feeling. And when she talked from her intellectual background, referring to ideas and philosophies he had never heard about, Sean laughed and called her a high-brow snob.

Tara was even more astounded at how Sean, who had happily shared housework and cooking as well as recreational pursuits before the wedding, seemed to change after they were married. She accused him of being a male chauvinist like his father, who went out to the footy and the pub with his mates while Sean's mother worked full time, held down two jobs, did the housework, mothered two kids and paid the bills. They were spending barely any time together. In alarm at her own bad judgment, Tara retreated from the relationship. Complaining that Tara was too cerebral, critical and closed, Sean used this to justify a series of one-night stands and an extramarital affair, which he kept secret from Tara but not his mates.

Despite a brief round of couple counselling, the marriage foundered within a year. Only once, on another two-week holiday together, did they manage to recapture some of the rapture of the early days of their relationship. But when they returned home, the old frustration resurfaced.

What had happened?

When Tara and Sean were *on holiday* they allowed themselves far more freedom to enjoy themselves. Their personal barriers dropped, they were able to accept each other unconditionally and each found the other a perfect partner. In these loving moments, they appeared as the other wanted them to be and not how they truly were. Once they were home, the constraints of their daily life and their conditioning clicked back in, and they were astonished at their differences.

What they discovered was that their *Holiday Characters* had fallen in love. Had they not been on holiday, neither of them would have been attracted to the other. Sadly, and with varying degrees of blame, they separated and went on with their lives.

A common charade

Tara and Sean aren't alone in this experience. We all have a number of Characters within us. There are scores more we can observe in our families and friends, colleagues, in movies or TV sitcoms that amount to a cast of thousands. They are sub-personalities, or parts of ourselves which appear automatically in certain situations. We may have different Characters on holiday, at work, at home, when driving, shopping or playing sport, or in any situation that requires a prescribed set of actions or behaviours. Our Characters are automatic in the sense that while we are 'in' a certain Character, we do not think consciously about what we are doing or how we are behaving.

For example, if we're visiting our parents after living on our own for some time, we might be annoyed if they still treat us as though we are still a child living under their roof. Still more disconcertingly, we might find *we* are acting in the same way we did then, even though we behave like independent adults in every other part of our lives. Characters are often automatic ways of behaving, depending on where we are and who we are with.

At work, our boss may consider we are a Desk Slave while our partner at home, who is privy to our sarcastic comments about office politics, sees us as a Strategic Game Player. Our parents may see us as a High Achiever or Loser, while our children may see us as their Heroes or Uncool. To an extent, the ways we behave with different people cement their ideas of who we are. We are then more likely to fall into that way of acting whenever we are with them.

We may not be aware that we behave differently with different people. We assume we are the same with everyone most of the time, while *others* behave differently towards us. While we might feel we are spontaneous, laid-back or just normal, it may actually be our personal cast of Characters, automatically rotating as needed.

Characters can be just one mask, or sometimes a series of masks, behind which we hide. They allow us to feel safe and unchallenged in certain situations. However, their behaviour is so automatic that they can prevent us from consciously running our own lives.

Sometimes, as with Tara and Sean, they can lead us into disasters.

2

Slipping into Character

The best way to identify that we are in a Character is when we can see that the way we are behaving around a certain person or situation is somehow *dictated* by that person or situation. Without realising it we slip into a conditioned way of acting that is a Character.

Characters are our unconscious reactions to repeated or intense situations that occurred in our past. Usually they developed at an early age, and they continue to operate in our adult lives because we are used to them and because they 'work' for us. They are so much a part of us we believe we *are* our Characters.

We think we are individual, but the same basic Characters are identifiable in many people. These Characters have the same agendas and illusions, the same thoughts, desires and fears. They can be picked out by a certain look, by their body language and clothes that reflect their self-image.

We tend to notice them in ourselves first when they stop working for us, when we feel unhappy or uncomfortable in specific situations around certain people. Whenever we feel we are behaving in a way that is not truly us, it's likely to be a Character that is driving our behaviour.

How a Character begins

A Character can be formed early in our lives when painful events leave a deep and lasting impression. The way we reacted at that time enabled us somehow to 'survive'. How our parents treated us, even if they were mostly caring and loving, the way they conducted themselves, and the expectations they placed on us all play their part in determining the nature of a Character.

If we've had early brushes with domineering authority figures, we can develop a Submissive or Compliant Character to help us cope. While this may help while we are small, dependent and vulnerable, in general it doesn't help us as an adult. Alternatively, if we hate being controlled, we might develop a Rebel Character. It might make us feel strong in certain situations, and this pattern may continue into adulthood even when inappropriate, where we wonder why everyone is in conflict with us and life is so difficult.

Conditioning

Conditioning occurs when specific behaviours receive a reward or positive reinforcement, leading to an increase in such behaviours. Negative reinforcement or punishment can also condition behaviour, in avoidance of what we perceive as preceding—or causing—the punishment.

If winning is important to our parents and they showed us their disappointment when we did not come first, this conditions us to do well to make them proud and impress the extended family. We get so used to it from an early age that we accept it as normal. We might develop a High Achiever Character—a Straight-A Student or a Star Athlete—to please our parents, or to prove early critics and detractors wrong. The Character might not reflect at all who we really are, or how we want to be.

Looking at Tara and Sean's Holiday Characters from this perspective, each of them had developed Workaholic Characters that operated most of the week at their jobs. Their Holiday Characters were the opposite. When not concerned with responsibilities and deadlines, they allowed themselves to let go. It made them feel a little drunk, and their judgment loosened accordingly.

There are other influences that create Characters. Our religious institutions and our national, cultural and genetic backgrounds are all significant factors. Our gender and our social and financial status can be important too, as can a city or rural upbringing, or even the local climate. A Character moulded in a cold northern climate, for example, where sunlight hours are short and not to be wasted, is conditioned to be purposeful and goal-orientated. A Character developed in a tropical climate, where siestas in the middle of the day are the norm, contrasts enormously. The evening meal is late and out of doors, and there's a relaxed attitude to work and punctuality. These and other conditioning elements are so much a part of our lives that we don't realise how much they shape us.

When childhood events are too painful, we suppress our memory of them. Often we only recall these hurts when similar situations arise. Sometimes, as we reflect on certain patterns in our lives and where these began, we recall unhappy situations we'd partly forgotten about. When we can step back and see how a certain Character behaves, we can often see where this survival behaviour came from. The great gift is that in seeing this as adults we are able to make better choices.

Hey little girl

The Little Girl is a Character we often see, and Maddie had one even though she is an astute businesswoman with her own consultancy. She was independent and brilliant as long as she was not in a relationship. When she was dating and it was getting serious, she changed from a mature, smart woman into a needy Little Girl. As a child she had developed a Little Girl Character to deal with the demands placed on her by her benevolent, but intrusive, father. The Character worked because her father approved of her more when she appeared sweet and innocent, when she asked for and followed his advice, when she accepted his generosity and was affectionately grateful. Having seen his alarm if ever she had ideas that were different to his, or when she tried to go her own way, she moulded herself to try to guarantee his love. Over time she automatically behaved submissively around him. Her father's approval became more important to her than her independence, and even her own idea of who she was. She became insecure and needy of his love.

The Little Girl Character was triggered in Maddie whenever she was in the presence of men like her father or any authority figure. In adult relationships, the Little Girl Character prevented her being an equal. Because she had disempowered herself, she had to resort to indirect, manipulative means to get what she needed and wanted. She deferred to the man's opinions, and she preferred to please him and fit in with his life than develop her own interests. Her life was moulded into his—a fact she only realised when her most recent love affair ended: his life continued as before, while hers changed radically, and even after they split up, her ex-partner's opinion of her still mattered more than her own.

The Little Girl Character is easy to pick. You might see her in the woman who smiles coyly and has a thin, high-pitched voice. She's excessively sweet. She twists her hair with her fingers and looks up through her lashes with lowered head. She uses covert manipulation, sexual games or tantrums to get what she wants. Frequently she craves attention to prove she is loved. If people consistently give in to her, the Little Girl Character becomes so automatic and entrenched that she may be quite unaware of how the Character takes over in her daily life, especially when she feels powerless. Famous examples include Marilyn Monroe and Princess Diana, both of whom used celebrity and public adulation to compensate for deep insecurities, while punishing themselves with self-destructive behaviour.

The Little Girl or the Little Boy may be created from a range of different family scenarios. Parents may have been distant or cold. They may have been dominating authority figures, whose love is conditional on prescribed behaviour. The youngest child in a family might adopt this role after being spoiled, or by feeling she can never measure up to the achievements of her siblings. Other Characters such as High Achiever, Mediator, Sports Star or Black Sheep may have been already taken by older brothers and sisters in the family. Often the only Character left for the youngest child is the Cute one.

Variations on the Little Girl or Boy are the Invalid/Chronically Ill, Scapegoat or Victim. An Invalid or a Victim Character develops when being sick or acting helpless are guaranteed means of getting attention or love, or being safe. In a Victim Character, fear can keep the person immobilised and tentative much of their life, long after the frightening influence has gone. Residual fear means we project the same expectation of danger or oppression everywhere, even in harmless situations, something experienced by any marginalised minority group within a society. A Scapegoat Character has somehow agreed to be the problem child in the family. This allows the other members to believe they don't have problems of their own because the focus of their attention is on the Scapegoat, who has yet again got into trouble.

What the real people inside these Characters have in common is that they all feel relatively powerless and compelled to fulfil a role that becomes expected of them.

Why can't my Little Girl Character just grow up?

The good news is that, with recognition and conscious effort, disempowered Characters like the Little Girl can mature. The Little Girl Character might fail to work if she meets someone who wants her to be more self-determined or take responsibility for herself. Alternatively, she might come to the realisation that by being the Pleaser she is no longer getting what she wants from a relationship, that her partner takes her for granted, is inconsiderate or not worthy of her over-accommodating ways.

When a woman becomes aware that the Little Girl no longer works for her, the real person within might be alarmed and dismayed, because for so long she has relied on the Character to keep her true Self hidden. She may begin to despise the Little Girl's automatic emergence whenever she is with fatherly men. The *real person within* is the key here. She is not the Little Girl Character but someone altogether different, someone she has yet to discover.

Growing out of a Character is like a butterfly emerging from a chrysalis.

3

Past trauma, present pain

The reason behind the automatic nature of our Characters is intriguing. Behaviour alone does not give the full picture. To change—to become more ourselves—we need to go deeper.

Twenty-year-old Rudy was upset when he came to see me. A few days before, he'd been parked at the beach with his gorgeous new girlfriend Leila, on a beautiful, moonlit night. He was in love and Leila was warm, smart and funny. Although he'd felt vaguely uneasy when they'd first arrived at the beach, he'd ignored it, looking forward to getting closer to his girl. Leila was showing him how much she wanted him too, when without warning something inside Rudy exploded and he pushed her away.

Rudy was furious, but didn't understand why. He got out of the car, intending to clear his head. Instead he found himself having a panic attack. His breathing became difficult and he felt feverish and cold by turns. The darkened beach and esplanade seemed full of flashing lights and distorted, threatening sounds. As he told me about it, his face was anxious and haunted. Not least of his concerns was that Leila now thought he was crazy.

Back we went through Rudy's past, gently peeling away layers of similar situations to see if we could source his unease. One by one Rudy experienced past incidents, discharging the emotion around them as he went. Eventually, he uncovered a situation he'd never remembered before.

Boy interrupted

It was his fifth birthday. He was at the same beach, on the same esplanade with his family on a Sunday afternoon. Rudy could hear the waves crashing on the sand and the wind in the pines. As he relived the smells of the salt-laden air, fish'n'chips, vinegar and sunscreen, they brought back memories of his early childhood. He could hear the excited screams and laughs of children playing in the background.

Rudy was riding his new BMX bike without training wheels for the first time. Momentarily he lost control and careened off the esplanade into the path of an oncoming bus. The bus screeched to a halt, knocking him from his bike. Rudy recalled seeing his body lying there on the road, unconscious and bleeding, as though he were floating some feet above his body, while frantic adults and stunned children hovered over him.

Though he was unconscious at the time, Rudy's brain recorded everything he could hear and feel at a subconscious level. It captured the impact of the collision, his body being thrown through the air and falling to hard asphalt. The memory was absorbed into the cells of his muscles, tissues, bones and organs. Rudy was aware of the bus driver as the man rushed to his side, saying, 'Oh my God, is he dead? Is he dead? I couldn't stop! He came out of nowhere, I didn't see him and I couldn't stop in time!' Rudy's unconscious mind had also absorbed the deep pain and shock the driver felt as he knelt by Rudy's side. He could make out frantic voices and footsteps as people came running towards him. All around him were voices full of fear asking what had happened, had the ambulance been called, was there a blanket to cover him, as the boy was in shock. Someone warned the onlookers not to move him in case he had a spinal injury. Rudy heard his mother's voice, full of guilt and terror, saying she'd *told* him to be careful, but he never listened, and *was he all right?* He heard someone say his bike was wrecked and would never be the same. Over these voices he heard the ambulance siren and then the calm, professional voices of the paramedics assessing him and recording vital observations as they transported his unconscious body in the wailing ambulance to the hospital.

As Rudy re-experienced in the session what had happened so long ago, his muscles were tense with the urgency that had underscored everything that day.

The morning after the accident Rudy recovered consciousness in hospital. He had a very sore head, concussion, a broken collarbone and leg, but he remembered nothing of the accident. His parents, feeling guilty and wanting to save him further trauma, simply told him that he'd fallen off his bicycle. They never referred to the accident in detail again.

Invisible influences

When Rudy returned to school, his teacher noticed some differences in the bright boy she'd grown fond of in his first few months. Rudy was now belligerent and moody. In the playground he would launch into fights and seemed unable to stop. In class he seemed distracted; he squinted to see the blackboard. When his teacher spoke to him Rudy appeared not to hear her. He was not the same boy. Medical tests failed to show any physical causes—his eyesight and his hearing were normal.

Rudy had to repeat his year and spent the rest of his time at school in the remedial class with developmentally disabled children. Strangely, his IQ was erratic. Sometimes it tested as high and sometimes below normal. He was diagnosed with Attention Deficit Hyperactive Disorder (ADHD) and prescribed Ritalin. Rudy believed he was stupid. He left school at fifteen, trying one job and apprenticeship after another, but never lasting long at anything. His Stupid Character was impatient and failed to finish tasks. He often misheard instructions and would get frustrated and rebellious. His insubordination to authority got him into trouble. His Stupid and Rebel Characters warred within him.

Rudy began to take drugs apart from the amphetamine-like Ritalin he had been prescribed. After a drug-induced psychotic episode, Rudy had a stretch in rehab. A few months afterwards, he met Leila and fell in love. He was apprenticed to a chef and things seemed to be looking up—until this recent, inexplicable incident.

The healing process

Some weeks of therapy ensued, during which Rudy re-experienced the accident and discharged the emotional pain as well as the cellular memory of it in his body. Reliving it consciously, with an adult's understanding, meant he was able to experience the incident more fully than he had as a child. What had been suppressed in his memory, he was now able to feel consciously and resolve.

Rudy's recollections were corroborated by his parents, who still felt some guilt over the incident. Rudy realised that certain words and phrases he'd heard while he was unconscious, which he'd been unable to make sense of, had exerted a powerful effect every time he found himself uncertain or threatened. Phrases such as 'I couldn't stop', 'I didn't see', 'he never listens', and 'it (his bike) will never be the same, it's wrecked', remained in Rudy's mind like post-hypnotic suggestions. They made him feel helpless and out of control, and this had become apparent in his inattention, impatience and belligerence at school.

The smell of salt in the air and the sound of waves, a siren or simply a screech of brakes in traffic also triggered feelings of helplessness, as he'd felt after the accident.

With Leila, just when he was opening his heart to more joy and love than he had yet experienced, these recollections and long-buried trauma at the very same beach had surfaced. Leila's physical closeness—like the ambulance paramedics attending him so long ago—had finally combined with all the other associations to spark his sudden, inexplicable fury with her that night.

Once the incident was discharged, Rudy was able to put the phrases and reactions to his injury into rational perspective. His life began to turn around. He returned to study, finished his schooling with high marks, began a degree in aviation engineering and is doing well. He and Leila are still together and thinking about marriage. His parents can barely believe he is the same person as the boy who was so difficult as a child and adolescent.

It's true that Rudy's not the same person.

The Stupid Character has gone and he's far more himself now.

4

The subtle forces that shape us

To understand how automatic reactions are triggered we need to go deeper still, beyond our physical bodies to the various layers in our energy field—our subtle bodies—and the intricate ways they interact with our behaviour. The subtle bodies that are concerned with Characters are the *etheric* or life-force body; the *astral* body, which deals with emotions and thoughts; and the *Egoic* body, vehicle of the Higher Self. Learning how these operate can give us the insight we need to become masters of our Characters.

Our subtle bodies are operating whether or not we are aware we are more than just our physical bodies. They are fields of life force, emotion, thought and spirit which inform us as long as we are alive.

We have many more subtle bodies than the two or three most of us will ever perceive. They are generally described as being in layers, but strictly speaking they're not separate like layers at all—more like amorphous fields of varying density, the finer of which interpenetrate the denser ones. It's as though the Egoic body, the largest we can feel or see with our human senses, is an enormous globule of water. Within that is a far smaller egg-shaped field of a fine network of sponge-like fibres—our astral body, province of thoughts and emotions. Within that is the etheric or life-force body— a smaller, denser sponge that follows the contours of our physical body. Within that sponge is the even denser physical body. Circulating through the whole structure is the 'water' of the Ego, spirit incarnate. Our astral body fully permeates the etheric and the physical, and the etheric fully permeates the physical. The significance of realising this aspect of the whole structure is that it's possible consciously to infuse the denser and more reactive parts of our bodies with the Ego or Higher Self simply by being aware that infinite light of spirit is always flowing through us.

The etheric body

The etheric body holds our life force and a bit more. The 'bit more' is like electricity: unseen except in its effects. Filling the physical body, it extends a little way out from the skin and we feel its effects as sensations of tingling, vibrations, tremors or shivers—like the feeling of 'someone walking over our grave'. In the etheric body we can experience vertigo or giddiness, or hot and cold sensations that are not measurable via a thermometer. The etheric body can perceive tangible feelings of pressure or weight that are frequently experienced as not quite, but *sort of*, physical. When our aware-ness extends into the etheric body, say in the twilight between sleep and waking, we sometimes feel it as an enveloping pillow, or feel we are as rotund as the Michelin Man. Subjectively our size is distorted, feeling tiny or huge.

We may perceive someone else's etheric body when we stare receptively at their physical body for a long time—such as when they are giving a speech, or when we are sitting in silent, still eye contact with them. It's a thinnish line of light that follows the contours of the physical body. It is elusive and amorphous enough for us to be able to dismiss it as an optical illusion.

When the person we are looking at is ill, their etheric body is a bit flat, like flattened fur on a cat. When people are healthy, it stands up like perpen-dicular fur several inches out from the physical body. In healers, etheric life force can radiate from their hands.

The etheric body interacts with the physical and the astral bodies. When we are healthy and have lots of life force, the etheric body acts as a buffer to our emotions so we are not so affected by them, but can rationalise or balance any emotional reaction. It's why people are often more emotional and more easily affected when they are ill, and can be more emotionally detached when they are healthy. There are exceptions, of course, but gener-ally this also means that our Characters have more control over us when we are out of balance physically than when we are healthy. If, as well as eating healthy food and getting enough sleep, we can increase the health of our etheric body by physical exercise, the lighter stagnant blocks in our energy can often be moved. On the other hand, as lighter blocks are discharged, deeper ones may surface. As a general rule, if something comes up in terms of our emotional reactions, it's a sign we're now strong enough to deal with its causes in the past.

The astral body

The astral body is perceived as a cloudy, egg-shaped field around the physical body, and can extend a metre or so from it. Sometimes with subtle vision we can perceive faint colours or brighter flashes. Some spiritual healers have attributed specific colours to specific emotions, but I think that to attribute a standardised meaning to colours in the astral body is a bit like attributing different kinds of lightning to the moods of God.

The astral body registers emotions and 'catches' thought waves through fine energetic structures similar to spider webs. It's a network made of something like electricity, which becomes more fixed through constant repetition of certain thought forms or mental habits. Our thought forms are energetic structures that can be caught and shared. People who spend time together often find their thoughts run synchronistically. A 'think tank' draws on this to generate ideas and spark inspiration, operating through a kind of catalytic thought contagion. The atmosphere of a university generates different thought patterns to a holiday cruise, a drama school, ballet performance or a jail.

If we are not particularly hungry and sit next to a stranger on a bus who is thinking about what they will prepare for their evening meal, we might find ourselves also thinking of food. We won't necessarily think of the same food as our fellow passenger, however. It is the *energy* of the thought and not necessarily its *content* that will be transmitted, and it is via the astral body that this happens.

We can also perceive someone's emotion through subtle vibrations. We can sense when there has been anger or rage expressed in a room shortly before we arrived there, or feel the sadness or fear in an empty hospital waiting room. If we are susceptible or if our boundaries are not strong, someone else's strong emotion can affect us more than we would like. Our astral body, again, is the medium through which this occurs.

The Egoic body

The most subtle of the energy bodies within the normal range of human perception is the Egoic body. The most definable thing about this body is the sense of ineffable 'presence'—we become aware of ourselves as spiritual beings, and at the same time of other spiritual beings. There are also perceptions of vastness, timelessness, varying qualities of light and levity, openness, compassion, love or joy. It is the body that is closest to Spirit.

When referring to Characters in this book, it is almost always the astral body, with its reactive thoughts and emotions, that is involved. The Egoic body is of a completely different composition to the astral body. When in the Ego we do not think—we *know*. It is beyond a mental state. Instead of reactive emotions, there are feelings which are unconditioned and unconditional. They are profound and timeless. There is the knowingness of far-reaching perception, deep understanding and love. There is a powerful sense of what is right, and this is not always conventional morality. Experientially, these feelings are so different to our normal, grasping, astral way of interacting with our environment that they require some getting used to.

When I talk about the Self rather than a Character, I am mostly referring to how we are when we are in the Egoic body. This is not quite what we feel when we believe we are being our *true selves*, but it is close. It is not at all the grasping ego of Freudian psychology. The Ego is spirit incarnate: the Egoic body is its vehicle. For our purposes here, it is synonymous with what many call the Higher Self. Above all, the Higher Self enables us to rise above emotional conditioning and psychological and physical trauma, and to rise above the biology of the 'selfish gene'. In many cases, Characters are distorted or pale reflections of the Higher Self. Sometimes they are so distorted that they barely correspond with the Higher Self—but they can lead us to it.

The Egoic body is significant for mastering our Characters and becoming our authentic Selves, because it epitomises potential. It is a far greater beingness into which we can grow.

Soul scars

It's astonishing how much our subtle bodies can reveal, though at first it's difficult to see what they are telling us. It's a bit like seeing the action of

The subtle bodies

An out-of-scale representation of the subtle bodies: Egoic (outer oval),
astral (smaller oval) and etheric (extending out from the human form).

centuries of wind in the honeycombed erosion in rocks. We can understand the past by seeing the results in the present.

The imprint of previous physical or emotional pain or trauma motivates many of our states of mind, emotions and reactions, years after such events. When Rudy was hit by the bus, he was left with mental and emotional scars in his astral body that could be triggered at any time. These scars are called *samskaras*, which is a Sanskrit word meaning 'scar' or 'trace' on our astral body. The word *samskara* also means 'motivator' in Sanskrit.

As long as our *samskaras* remain unresolved, the entire astral body is charged and under stress, always able to be provoked. Some of us have so many *samskaras* we are virtually the walking wounded. Most of our *samskaras* are buried wounds that prompt us to be evasive or to react in certain ways to compensate for our wounding. We do this without thinking so we can cope with particular situations. Unless we deal with our *samskaras*, our unconscious behaviour will continue.

Samskaras can be very powerful. Once formed, they keep a Character 'locked in', continuing to replay the same Character whenever certain provoking or threatening elements are present. Even though we want to behave differently, when a *samskara* is triggered, we end up reacting the same way over and over. The Office Mouse who can't say no to the extra work her colleagues pile on her might end up on permanent stress leave when her in-tray becomes so full there is no chance she will ever catch up. A Pleaser Character, the Office Mouse simply wants to be liked, and so she is locked into behaviour that she believes will achieve that. Her original *samskaras* might have been a consistent lack of love in her childhood home, combined with high expectations and criticism from her parents. She's had so much disapproval in her childhood, she will do anything to avoid it. So she keeps on making unrealistic agreements until she gets sick and has an excuse to stop. Only when the *samskaras* at the basis of this Character are discharged can she have the courage to rest in her own approval of herself and say no.

How *samskaras* are formed

A *samskara* is created as a result of an emotional wound or physical injury that has an emotional component—such as a sudden shock, loss or fright, or even shame or an unjust accusation. Though they are energetic wounds in the subtle body, we can sometimes feel *samskaras* as an ache or sharp pain, a blockage or a void. We usually feel them years later, when there is no apparent physical cause, but when the *samskara*'s charge in the astral body resonates with a triggering factor in the environment. At the moment of the wounding, however, they won't be immediately apparent: at times of extreme distress, our attention is usually in getting to safety or covering our hurt, and the actual pain is blocked from our consciousness just as shock blocks physical pain.

There are some similarities with how our central nervous system deals with physical injury. When we get a physical hurt, our body's defences immediately isolate the wound with a flow of lymph, making it numb while repair begins. It helps us survive. Blocking the wound from our immediate awareness allows us to get to safety, motivated by primitive fear but unaffected by pain for a varying period of time. Endorphins flood our brain, and we function automatically until these recede.

A *samskaric* wound has similar effects to a physical wound. There is a numbed, physical site for it, which is often in the same spot as a previous injury. It's where there is a weakness or breach in our energy field, within and around the physical body. It's difficult, however, to discern an energetic wound from a physical pain. In some of us our original wound is in our heart, and can be felt as a physical pain when we are distressed. It's what we feel when we talk of a 'broken heart'. In others, the original wound is in our belly, solar plexus or other spots in the physical body. We know it because it's where we usually feel pain, congestion or discomfort when something happens to upset us.

A telling example is when we suffer a bereavement—which most of us feel first in our hearts. At the death of a loved one, it's normal to become emotionally numb for a period of time. Endorphins released by shock make us so from the moment we receive the news. In this case, it's common to act almost normally, even though we don't feel normal at all. People close to us usually comment on how 'brave' we are, or how well we are taking it. Four to twelve weeks after a bereavement, it's also common to start crying with no apparent cause. This happens when the endorphins have finally receded and our brain and central nervous system have to deal with the unbuffered impact of our loss. Our heart aches. It even feels broken. We cry at the drop of a hat. We lose our keys or the thread of the conversation. We think we must be going nuts. Yet it's normal. Crying at this stage is healing and it doesn't last forever. It's also the time when those same close friends, who don't know about endorphins, tell us with great concern that we 'should be over it by now'. But grief takes as long as it takes and has its own wisdom, giving us compassion and empathy. Sooner or later, time gives the loss perspective and we become more recognisably ourselves once more, though deepened, and capable of more profound understanding.

If we suppress or deny grief, it becomes compacted and harder to let go as time goes on. The physical pain around the heart might increase. Later sad experiences compound the congestion and add the weight of their significance. When this *samskara* cluster is triggered it becomes unbearable. It creates the Grief Character—unable to feel the grief fully because of resistance, and unable to let it go, truly stuck in a numbing emotion. We can make it so much easier on ourselves if we let the natural grief process take its course. Cry when you're sad, and let the sadness go when enough time has passed for you to feel you can.

The *samskaric* consequence of devastating loss is that we might avoid becoming close to anyone else in the future, for fear of re-experiencing the same pain. The *samskaric* imprint on our astral body links any pain in our present with that of the past. If, like most of us, we have not discharged past pain, that increases present hurts. On the other hand, when we have discharged the pain of the past, through experiencing it without resistance and letting it go, we only have to deal with what is happening now. Without the complication of past wounds, those of the present can be far more quickly resolved and healed. We can move on without being *unnecessarily* affected. We are far more resilient.

Connecting to spirit

Our true Self, the real us, is our higher consciousness. This is the Ego, spirit incarnate, that resides in the Egoic body. Because we are so caught up in the emotions and thoughts of the astral body, we are rarely aware of this body except in the stillness of meditation or in the profound, universal letting go that can accompany the grief of great loss. It connects us to something greater than ourselves, to other spiritual beings and to our eternal existence. We can become aware of a transpersonal level of being, one beyond our purely personal concerns. It enables us to take responsibility for our lives, to grow into who we truly are, no matter what past events or situations may have diverted that development.

In a *samskara*, consciousness is driven out by the impact of the injury, as happens in a physical wound. The astral body, with its compacted emotions from both past and present now out of proportion, takes the place of higher consciousness and makes it more difficult to connect to the Egoic body and our true Self. Around our wounding is a layer of unconsciousness, formed in much the same way as an oyster coats an irritating piece of grit with nacre. An energy block results and our etheric or life energy stagnates in this spot. A *samskara* thus feels like a hole or vacancy in our energy—an *emptiness of spirit*, as Dr Samuel Sagan, founder of the Clairvision School of Meditation in Sydney, so eloquently describes it.

The pain of the wound and its emotional content are encapsulated, isolated from consciousness, replaced by deadened scar tissue. Sometimes we can operate as though everything is fine for years—as in the case of

Maddie and her Little Girl Character, which functioned automatically *in the place of* the real Maddie for much of her life. Only when the automatic *samskaric* reactions come to our consciousness by causing more pain in our present life can we address them and resolve them, as seen in the story of Olivia's Bad Girl Character, below.

Blasts from an uncomfortable past

Olivia's past relationships were 'all bad', she said. She was devilishly attracted to bad boys. She went to jelly at the sound of a Harley, the smell of a leather jacket, or the look of dark hunger in the eyes of a stranger in a bar. She was drawn to danger and had an unswerving knack for picking men who used and abused her. But Olivia was also tired of finding her heart in pieces after every encounter. She would vow to put her attention on the decent men who were attracted to her, only to find that she had not the slightest interest in them. The chemistry just wasn't there.

Together we pieced together her repeating patterns, going backwards from her most recent disaster to her first relationship. Her father had been abusive and violent, a drunken, angry man who belonged to a biker gang, and who left the family when she was nine. Her older brother had bullied her and for five years had forced her into sexual 'games' with his friends.

Olivia's early *samskaras* took away her trust of males of all ages. Her self-esteem was continually eroded until she believed abuse was all that she deserved. She identified herself as a Slut or Bad Girl Character and behaved accordingly. This was a feisty, spitfire Character until several brutal encounters broke it down and it devolved into an Abused Girlfriend Character, similar to a Battered Wife. As an adult, even though she did not consciously attract abuse, it seemed that abusive men recognised her vulnerability and sought her out. She was unable to resist, as though hypnotised.

Olivia's relationship patterns illustrate the structure of *samskaras* and how they continue to function after they are formed. The original wounding is surrounded by a layer of unconsciousness, but the wound itself sends out a vibration of the energy frequency that caused it. This resonates with any similar energy in the environment, ranging from an identical energy to its opposite. In Olivia's case, her ability to be hurt attracted the opposite—an abusive energy in men—over and over again. It could equally attract losers and victims to be her friends. Until she saw the complete pattern, much later in therapy, she was unaware of this subtle chemistry in action.

Each successive abusive interaction causes another *samskaric* layer to form on top of the first, with layers of unconsciousness in between. Imprinted with each of the *samskaras* are associated sounds and smells. In Olivia's case, there was the insolent, macho 'look' of certain men, so like her father and brother. When Olivia came across these associations in her environment, they resonated within her astral body, awakening the automatic programming in her *samskaras* which misidentified emotional intensity as passion. Her physical body and her sexuality were conditioned to respond, even against her conscious will. When Olivia felt hypnotically drawn to dangerous men, she really was in a hypnotic trance. She was literally being pulled through the unconscious layers in the uppermost *samskara* to the place where she would be hurt, once again.

Samskaras are emotional land mines buried within us.

Defusing land mines

Defusing a *samskara* involves a gentle, patient exploration of the components of each layer in reverse chronological order. This is best done shortly after the *samskara* has been triggered—particularly when the reaction is inappropriately intense, as in Rudy's case. The triggering of the reaction, and an awareness that it is out of proportion to the situation, indicates our psyche is ready and strong enough to address the underlying *samskara*. Paradoxically, the time of greatest pain also gives the opportunity for the greatest awareness and wisdom. It's when old, ineffective patterns of behaviour are obvious to us, letting us know it's time for a change.

In a session, clients will often feel sleepy as they approach a painful *samskara*. It's because they are going through the unconscious layer that encapsulates every wound, a state that equates to a hypnotic trance where the rational mind is suspended. It is important not to succumb to the soporific energy of this stage and fall asleep, but gently to persist, to keep opening to the emotion with full consciousness.

Among the transpersonal techniques that I use is Inner Space Interactive Sourcing, or ISIS, developed by meditation teacher and author Dr Samuel Sagan. It is not a hypnotic technique. It does enable an altered state of consciousness where the body is relaxed, but unlike hypnosis there is no guided imagery and no suggestions are made to change what the client feels or sees. Clients are not asked to use their imagination as in purely mental techniques. Going deeply into the inner self, the client can bring the light of their own consciousness to areas of the unconscious mind, gently revealing things that have been suppressed, either intentionally or instinctively. The deep state of awareness in ISIS connects us to our Higher Self and so is more profound than our usual mental state. It enables a resolution and release of painful memories simply by becoming conscious of them at this deep level.

In a session, when we persist through the unconscious layer and allow ourselves to be led by the emotional pain of the *samskara* into its core, we re-experience the wounding without the shock of the initial reaction, but with a deeper, more mature consciousness. We can see or hear the thought patterns of any Character that was 'born' then and how it habitually feels, separate to how *we* actually think and feel. It is here that a Character's scripts and programming are found. We can bring more understanding, resilience and wisdom to it. We can put it into perspective and we can deal with it in a way that we were not able to do at the time of the wounding. We can reclaim the empty space from which we were excluded by the *samskara* and become whole. In the safety and trust of the therapist's room, we can relax into the situation completely. Old, intense pain and unresolved emotion can then be experienced and let go, without incurring further *samskaras*. When, like Rudy, a client can experience a *samskara* fully and without resistance, it is discharged forever.

5

Messages that resonate

Knowing how Characters are formed helps us change them, as does observing how they operate in our lives. Except in unusual circumstances, one single *samskara* is not enough to create a Character. Normally, they are made of a cluster of *samskaras,* a number of conditioning wounds.

Hidden laws of attraction

As we saw with Olivia, the vibration of our first *samskara* attracts a similar energy, and more *samskaras* are formed in layers on top—attraction and layering being one way the energy of the astral body functions. Characters are difficult to shake because *samskaras* are made of *astral* matter, which resonates on—and amplifies—a particular frequency of thought or emotion in the astral body.

For example, if a *samskara* is based on fear, we emit the vibrational frequency of fear through the astral body. Through resonance, this in turn attracts more fearful energy, or its predatory opposite. It can also generate this energy in others. It's much like what happens if we're afraid of dogs and unexpectedly meet one. Our fear transmits through smell to the dog's keen olfactory sense. This triggers fear in the dog's own body through astral resonance and it barks defensively. We react with more fear to this apparent aggressive attack, and so on.

As humans, we usually only register the smell of fear subliminally, that is, below our conscious awareness. But *resonance* in our astral bodies means that any fear we sense in others is likely to awaken the powerful echo of a past, forgotten event in which we ourselves were scared. We then react fearfully, quite out of proportion to the actual present event. In a primitive instinctual reaction to fearful energy, some people become aggressive, just as a dog will.

The opposite energy also comes into play here. So, an aggressive mugger or violent rapist will look for a person who has a fearful Victim energy. Weak energy in others makes the attacker even more angry, in a neat compensation for the weakness they despise in themselves.

This was the case for Ben, whose older brothers bullied him constantly at home. Hating himself for his pathetic Loser Character, which cried and curled up in a ball to protect himself rather than fighting back, Ben found it was a different situation at school. Coming across a child who was smaller and more vulnerable than himself, Ben acted out exactly the bullying behaviour his brothers had used with him for years. The power he felt to inflict pain and reduce another child to tears was exhilarating and addictive. In actual fact, in his Bully Character Ben was punishing the Loser Character within himself, while projecting the Loser onto the smaller boy.

The health or otherwise of our etheric body directly affects the amount of energy we, and our different Characters, can access. Even one *samskara* can cause a stagnant block in the normal energy flows of our physical and etheric bodies, and this, too, can sometimes be seen or sensed.

It is not only people who resonate or transmit a particular 'vibe' or energy: this can happen at the level of organisations too.

Catching the corporate vibe

Ravi and Sol were friends and business partners whose small computer business did relatively well until a fire destroyed their shop, all their stock and files. To regain some capital to start again, they both began working for a major telecommunications company. Ravi did well and was soon promoted, but Sol was overlooked and, eventually, his contract was not renewed. Sol was resentful, since he'd worked as hard as his friend, was more experienced and, in his own opinion, more talented.

Sol often had trouble with employers. He had a Rebel Character which was prone to asking prickly questions and doing his own thing rather than following guidelines. In the business he had shared with Ravi, he had been the leader, the visionary and the one who took risks. Ravi, on the other hand, had a Follower Character which adopted the values of those of higher status around him. He had been content to follow Sol's lead in their own business, and was now happily moving higher through the telecommunications company. Sol accused him of selling out. Ravi had no idea what Sol was talking about. They had encountered the telecom meme.

Memes: the astral body of an organisation

The meme, or prevailing culture of any large business, company or organisation, derives from the accepted way of thinking practised by top management, which is then filtered down through its hierarchy. It's something we can become aware of when we first begin working for a new organisation, join a club, or enrol in a school or college. It is through our astral body that the flavour of the meme is subtly discernible. Apart from any openly stipulated rules and regulations, there are tacitly acceptable ways of behaving, unspoken prohibitions and taboos. Those new employees or members who fit or are able to adapt to an organisation's meme, like Ravi, will do well, as though protected by a benevolent higher force. Those who are not able to adapt, or who consciously or unconsciously rebel against the hierarchy, will often feel they have been chewed up and spat out. Such was Sol's experience.

A meme is the astral body of an organisation, maintained by conscious absorption of the values, ideas and emotional tone of those working there. Each organisation attracts and moulds Characters that fit its particular meme, and ejects those who do not.

Memes operate within family groups, as well as any social, political, educational or health institution. This was something high school teacher Anne found when she transferred from a privileged boys' private academy to a multicultural co-educational one in the inner city. The wealthy school turned out many of the city's professional elite in law, medicine, finance and business. Career advancements for graduates were based on an old boys' network with the same elitist attitudes as the school. Despite official proclamations to the contrary, an undercurrent of racism and misogyny ruled.

As one of the few female teachers at the school, Anne suffered marginalisation from the teaching hierarchy as well as outward indifference from the students, even though her classes achieved higher academic results than many others. In contrast, she found the meme of the inner-city school to be egalitarian and multicultural, and the staff caring, community-minded and supportive. This school produced excellent achievers in the arts as well as science, medicine and the helping professions, and Anne felt far more appreciated. Ironically, only a few months after she transferred, she was inundated with requests for private tutoring from her former students at the elite school.

Growing out of a meme

Karen was thrilled to be hired as cabin crew by an international airline, and maintained her enthusiasm for five years until internal restructuring meant her work conditions and pay went down, while the airline's expectations of its staff increased. Depressed feelings led her to therapy, where she uncovered a long-maintained Pleaser Character.

Psychometric testing by service and hospitality companies routinely target Pleaser Characters, because they are happy to be of service, often do far more than is required to keep other people happy and are frequently loath to stand up for themselves when unfairly treated by an employer. Naturally this is good for business. Karen remembered the pre-selection test had many questions along the lines of 'Would you go out of your way to give a passenger good service?' and 'What matters more to you when on duty: a passenger's comfort or yours?' Karen had once returned an expensive camera, left behind on the plane, to a passenger, delivering it in person late at night to his hotel in a foreign city. She'd even hailed a taxi in the pouring rain to do it, but received no thanks or monetary compensation for her above-and-beyond service.

After working on her Pleaser Character for a few weeks, I asked Karen how she would now deal with such a situation. She said she'd label the camera, leave it with the airline's Lost and Found, and possibly leave a message at the passenger's hotel to let him know. It was still professional and courteous service, just no longer a Pleaser's automatically over-accommodating behaviour. Over time, she became more assertive. Karen found she no longer fitted the meme but hesitated to leave, unsure of the viability of an idea she had for a business of her own. Shortly afterwards the company's rumour-mill circulated a completely untrue story that Karen had been 'inappropriately intimate' with passengers. She was sacked, and wished she had been more proactive and left earlier.

Memes are like that, often punishing Characters for going too far in any direction.

If we wish to operate within a meme in a healthy manner we need to ascertain what that particular meme is. In a business, what are the company's stated values? What are the hidden aspects of working there? Much can be gleaned from any candid comments made by people who work there. Initial interviews with potential bosses can also inform you of the kinds of conditions—not explicitly stated—that will operate when you are hired. Will you be required to behave differently to your values? What will you be required to sacrifice? Will their work ethic mesh with your own? If so, you may be able consciously to ride the meme and further your own goals at the same time as serving the aims of the company, giving a win–win outcome.

However, it's supremely easy for a meme to swallow us whole. And even if a general meme fits us, an opportunistic meme that sweeps through a company on a tornado of vicious supposition, disapproval or jealousy can eject us regardless.

6

Spotting a Character

The previous chapters have examined how information can resonate with us on so many different levels—from the subtle emanations of our etheric, astral and Egoic bodies, to the memes generated by corporate organisations and educational institutions.

We have also seen how *samskaric* wounds on our astral bodies can determine the Characters we later adopt.

As we first saw in Chapter 2, before we can change a Character that is impeding our progress or preventing us being true to our Higher Self, we need to observe the signs that tell us when we're in a Character.

One sure sign is when we feel our behaviour is following a script—and a fairly melodramatic one at that. It feels like there is a well-worn and familiar groove to the emotions involved, the words we say and the reactions we have. It's a pattern we have followed before. And, even though that behaviour has become our normal habit, it feels fake.

Another indication we are in Character is that we may not behave in a way that is appropriate to the situation. Time and again we watch ourselves making a situation worse and feel powerless to stop. Whenever we feel reluctant to be in a particular person's company because we feel out of control around them, or feel our behaviour determined *by* them, it's likely our Characters are involved, taking over when we would least like.

You may have met someone new and not known how to behave because the Character he is using is not one of your normal repertoire. That person may appear to shift Characters rapidly, resulting in a great deal of confusion as to what Character you 'should' be in. Ultimately, you end up disempowered and confused in your Stupid Character, with little chance of finding a way out of it.

The first time Darren met his girlfriend's parents was just such an occasion. Wanting to make a good impression, he tried too hard and made some quick assumptions. As he entered the house he noticed stuffed animal head trophies stacked in the hallway. Greeting the father, he pretended an enthusiasm for hunting, only to find that the heads had belonged to his girlfriend's grandfather, recently deceased. Her father was actually a peaceful man opposed to such bloodthirsty pursuits and the trophies were being sent elsewhere. Long after Darren and the girl were married, his father-in-law considered Darren was a gun buff and foolish, to boot. All attempts to reverse his opinion met with failure.

Another sign we are in a Character is when we believe we are being ourselves, yet others feel that we are not being genuine or they misunderstand our motives. This is tricky. Are they looking at us through their Characters? Are both parties in Characters? Who is really there?

I just need some space!

A helpful way to identify different Characters in ourselves and others is by their amount of personal space. Our sense of personal space is a function of our astral body. It's not only a crowded lift that makes most of us uncomfortable when it comes to sharing our personal space with strangers. Each of us has a certain area around us that is *our* personal space, and we can feel uncomfortable when it is invaded by someone else coming too close, uninvited. The amount of personal space that we feel comfortable sharing varies, depending on who we are with and how familiar we are with them.

With loved ones, our space *expands* in a relaxed fashion, and we include them in our space. We tend to *contract* our space if we feel threatened, condensing and concentrating all our fearful or hostile emotions into a tiny area immediately around us or even inside us. Naturally, this makes us highly uncomfortable, so we want to get away from the person or situation as quickly as possible.

Each Character has its own comfort zone of personal space which has crystallised over time into a rigid containment. Fearful Characters tend to exclude others from their small space, while a Jovial or High-Status Character often has a large space and can include others in it. While we may move our own spatial boundaries according to which Character we are in, as long as we are in a specific Character that Character's boundaries are fixed.

Am I invisible?

Sandy complained that whenever she was at a shop counter she was ignored and other shoppers were always served first. A recent incident left her fuming and considering acts of violence to get noticed. She had been standing at a counter for some time without being served. Another customer came up behind her with some purchases, and the shop assistant immediately stopped what he had been doing and reached *around* Sandy to get the second customer's goods.

Sandy's space was so small and constricted that the impact she made on people was minimal. To all intents and purposes she was invisible. It made her feel she had to be loud and aggressive to be noticed, and for Sandy that would take more energy than she had. Once Sandy learned that assertiveness is not aggression, and that she could assert her rights without losing her temper or raising her voice, she was able to speak up and expand her space.

The reason Sandy's personal space was so small was that most of the time she felt others vampirised her space, overwhelming her with their energy or draining her with their problems. To keep others out, she contracted her space and tried not to be noticed. She was surprised to realise that this had actually worked, though not as she had hoped—strangers treated her as though she was invisible, while those close to her took advantage of her meekness.

Much practice in expanding her space helped change this.

SPACE EXPANSION EXERCISE

Beginners
___

Make sure you're in a quiet place where you will not be disturbed. In the beginning it helps if you close your eyes for this exercise. You might like to get a friend to read it out and take you through it. It's important not simply to visualise or imagine each stage in a purely mental way, but to the best of your ability to feel or sense your space as it expands. Only proceed to the next stage if you can truly expand to the one you are in. No rushing, no effort. Simply allow the natural, gentle expansion of your space in its own time. If you find you are trying too hard, stop, go back gently to the solar plexus and begin again, using intention but no effort.

1. Sitting comfortably with eyes closed, put your attention in your solar plexus. Feel a warmth there, or perhaps for you it is a density, or a glow of light.

2. When you can feel the warmth, density or glow, relax, allow that sensation to spread, radiating from the solar plexus through your whole body. You might feel a subtle pulsing throughout your body as you do this, or you might not. Either is okay.

3. When you have a sense of the warmth, density or glow throughout your entire body, become aware of the space just *around* your body. You might feel a tingling here, or you might not. Either is fine.

4. When you have a sense of your energy expanded to the space just around your body, become aware of the 'egg' around your body. This is your personal space, about a metre or so around your physical body. Allow your energy consciously to fill the 'egg' around your body. It may begin to feel a little denser to you. If not, that's okay.

5. Take a moment to observe how it feels to fill the 'egg' around your body with your conscious presence. Most people describe this as feeling safe or comfortable.

6. Become aware of the room you are in. You may open your eyes slowly, or you may leave them closed. Allow your space gently to expand to fill the room. To help, without moving your body, sense-feel the walls, furniture, ceiling, windows and floor. With practice, the entire room will feel like 'your space', safe, and comfortable. Let your body remember the feeling so you can re-create it whenever you wish.

---

7. If you are doing this with a friend, become aware of how it feels to have your friend in your space. If you are alone while you do this exercise, as soon as you feel confident, try it in a bus or train station, a shop, walking down the street or meeting a friend. See how your expanded space increases your awareness. See how it affects how you feel, how people respond to you and you to them. Are there places where your space instinctively contracts? Is this appropriate—how you would like it to be? What are the differences between expanding your space in a natural setting and a built-up area?

---

8. Practise contracting and expanding your space until you can do it at will. No effort, no rush, just allow your space to expand.

Watch this space . . .

Because it's often easier to notice space issues in others than in ourselves, you might see it operating in your friends or colleagues. You might find a Character or two whose actions are determined by the amount of space they allow themselves or others.

A Victim Character has little personal space and feels as much a prisoner to that small space as to the situation around him. A Flirt Character has more space and tantalisingly plays with other people's space while still clearly defining his own boundaries. A Big Boss Character has quite a bit of personal space, and is likely to appropriate others' space as well, making them feel that they have even less personal space when he is near them.

Our space can expand and contract, depending largely on where our attention needs to be. For example, a Teacher Character expands her space in the classroom to make sure she reaches every member of the class. Her attention is over the whole class, even when she has her back to them while writing on the board, or explaining something just to one student while standing next to him. Back in the staffroom, however, she will often contract her space to just around her desk. It allows her fewer distractions as she gets on with preparing lessons or marking, and usually means she is noticed by fewer people and is not interrupted as much. If she needs to announce something to the whole staffroom, she will once more expand her space, to fill the room. The Character, however, is unaware she is doing it, and so in situations unrelated to teaching might be unable to expand her space. Even in the classroom, when kids cluster around her desk, the Teacher Character might feel overwhelmed and contract her space while reminding the kids to stop crowding her. At this point, her authority is diminished or lost.

In some extreme cases, our space cannot easily be expanded or contracted. A child in an abusive home situation might be conditioned to contract her space to the point where she finds it difficult to expand it. Her contracted space means she has little presence and little power over her environment. Having little personal space, she doesn't learn boundaries in a way that a child in a loving, functional family should. This applies also to neglected children, who are similarly conditioned to be abused or neglected further. A child in an indulgent family situation might never learn boundaries because she is given too much space—and may even learn manipulative or bullying techniques involving taking over the personal space of others, and abusing them without really being aware of what she is doing.

My space or yours?

It's intriguing to realise that we can give away our personal space, and that this is an infallible indicator that we are in a Character—and that the other person usually is, too! It helps to realise that somehow we are *agreeing* to give away our space. Sometimes this awareness is enough for us to give ourselves our space back.

It's an evolving journey. At first we might believe others vampirise our space, or dump on us without reason. If we've grown out of or are resisting Victim, we may then develop a bristly or feisty Bully Character to counter any space invasions, one that is bigger than those around us. However, once we've mastered the tricky boundaries of personal space, we're not affected by the astral energy of others or by their emotional fall-out. We'll still be aware of others' emotional states. It's just that we will be able to leave their problems with them instead of inappropriately taking them on board.

When we are in our Egoic body with its limitless space, we have no need to vampirise others or defend our own space. We can begin to recognise others in their Ego as well and we will be attracted to them in preference to people in their Characters. We'll know by a feeling we sense in them of expansiveness and complete acceptance, like being in love.

When we can allow ourselves to resonate with someone in their Ego, it has a transformational effect on us too. We begin to resonate on a higher level. Life becomes more interesting and fun as a result, while the deep connections we can make with others have none of the reactive or manipulative games that Characters play.

Energy to burn

As well as observing the amount of space it occupies, we can tell much about a Character by tuning into its energy. We can feel someone else's energy, like an emotion, as heavy or light, fluid or fixed, concentrated or scattered, explosive or implosive, dense or diffused, or any degree in between. High physical energy—meaning very active, enthusiastic or purposeful energy— is generally lighter than low, inactive energies characterised by inertia, and it moves/vibrates faster.

Characters with a high energy level are naturally more active. Their high energy also helps them persist on a chosen path, achieve goals and operate effectively in their lives. On a professional level, classic high-energy Characters include Nurse, Policeman, Sports Star, Jovial Host, Doctor, Lawyer, Teacher, Coach, Manager, Coordinator/Planner, Therapist and Preacher. Low-action Characters with no specific professional function include Victim, Invalid, Doormat, Battler and Couch Potato. On occasion, low-action Characters can co-exist with high-energy ones in the same person.

Doctor Allman's zoo

A medical doctor in his surgery answers his phone in his Business Character's voice, then switches to Poor Me when he hears it is his Career

Woman wife, who wants him to look after the kids while she has a meeting after work. His next caller is a patient, with whom he is his breezy Doctor Character, patronising and impatient with her anxiety about her upcoming operation. Then he rings a colleague to re-arrange their squash game, taking the jocular tone of a Competitive Sportsman Character. When the kids arrive at the surgery he plays the Stern Father, telling them to behave themselves while he sees his last patient. In none of these automatic Characters is the doctor himself genuinely or fully present.

A person with a Professional Character often behaves in a different way when out of uniform or their professional environment, say, doing the shopping. At work, their clothing, such as a doctor's white coat, helps define their profession and status. They may not even realise what effect their uniform and place of work have on an energetic level. In uniform or behind a badge, a Professional Character gives herself more space and a higher action level. When in uniform their energy is lighter because it is 'carried' by the meme of their profession.

Is it a bird? Is it a plane? It's Supermum!

Sharon had three kids under seven and prided herself on her efficiency as a mum. She always made her two school-age kids nutritious lunches, brought baked goods to playgroup with her youngest, and her well-behaved kids always looked clean and well dressed. She was active in the P&C and school canteen, and took part in the parental remedial reading program. Sharon thrived on being busy and loved her life. When she went back to work part time, she had no doubt that her organisational skills would carry her through all the extra time pressure she now had to deal with. But within six months she was diagnosed with clinical depression.

To make time for everything, Sharon's Supermum Character had taken over, prioritised her activities and jettisoned some, including her daily laps at the pool and her twice-weekly yoga class. Supermum reasoned that her family was the most important thing, and for that she had to sacrifice her 'me' time. Supermum also reasoned that now she was working so hard, a little drink now and then would help relieve her stress. A little drink now and then soon turned into many and often. Soon she was not sleeping, and doing frantic spates of housework during the night. Crunch-time came one weekend when she couldn't stop crying. Meanwhile Supermum was furiously telling her she was hopeless as a mother, and beating her up for not being perfect.

It took some weeks for Sharon to take her life back from the demands and recriminations of Supermum. She arranged to share some of the child-care with her willing husband, and resumed her exercise. She stopped her excessive drinking. Now she is as enthusiastic as ever, and her life is much more balanced.

To help balance her life, Sharon enlisted the help of a previous Charac-ter: Party Girl. In the past, Party Girl's wild excesses included the usual party drugs, alcohol and periods of irresponsibility, for which Sharon would after-wards feel ashamed and guilty. For some years, Supermum had managed to banish Party Girl, but every now and then Party Girl had emerged as a release valve to relieve the stress in Sharon's life.

In Sharon's new life, she allows Party Girl to come out when she needs her, but this time it is Sharon taking over rather than the Character. She has fun, she relaxes and she returns to her responsibilities refreshed.

I'm mad as hell!

It is very easy to see that anger has an explosive energy. Who doesn't im-mediately relate to the phrases, 'She was spitting chips!' or 'He went ballistic!'? Beneath the pyrotechnics, however, an Angry Character's energy is relatively fixed and solid, because anger creates a hard energetic ridge around the body. The Angry Character usually wants to stop something, so she unconsciously creates an energetic buffer zone or barrier around herself to stop unwanted influences reaching her, which may or may not be effective. Unfortunately this protective wall will also make it difficult for her to communicate: she feels she has to shout over it to make herself heard. She might feel this barrier belongs to those who oppose her. In attempting to break through, she may even resort to violence when she fails to communicate verbally.

Dousing the flames

If you've ever watched an interaction between an angry customer and a customer service staff member well trained in conflict resolution, you may have observed something fascinating. The furious customer approaches the staff member to voice his complaint. The staff member keeps eye contact with the customer, faces him bodily with arms relaxed and silently lets him vent his spleen until the problem has been fully communicated. She nods whenever he makes a point, and matches his communication with a sober, attentive face that lets him know she is listening and taking him seriously. Her first response will be to ask how she can help or fix the problem. His reply to this will be somewhat calmer, because she is not blocking him by trying to minimise his problem or quieten him down.

Energetically, she is not resisting his explosive manner as most of us might, nor is she trying to control him from a personal fear of confrontation. Focused on a solution, she is listening to *what* he is saying and not reacting to *how* he is saying it. His attempt to get through the energetic barrier of his anger is helped when she simply accepts the communication. As a result, the barrier drops, and they can work on finding a solution that suits them both. However, an Angry Character, as opposed to just a furious person, might be so stuck in anger that he barely calms down, wanting instead to find more reasons to fight.

The many faces of fear

When we feel fear in any form we might automatically contract our space in a Fearful Character who uses various defence mechanisms. The Fearful Character may lack confidence and have a low self-esteem, and in many cases this will show as the low-profile approach of self-effacement, a reluctance to stand out or be noticed in case he is ridiculed, or avoidance. Or it may entail a chronic suspicion and scepticism of others' motives. On the flipside there may be an elaborate camouflage, so-called superiority complexes or aloofness which are designed to distance us from the perceived danger, an appearance of invulnerability in an attempt to dissuade attack, an aggressive or hypercritical behaviour pattern, or more consciously, the counterphobic's headlong rush to face his fears by doing the very thing that terrifies him most.

In terms of energy, fear is a dispersal as well as a contraction. The person feels he has less space, but at the same time is literally scattering his energy. His attention gets dispersed too. He has lost his focus and his centredness, so he does not behave with much presence of mind. He is too scattered to notice things and therefore his memory retention is poor. He is so busy trying to maintain his protective buffer zone that he does not take in what is being said to him unless it fits his fearful world view.

When we are in a Fearful Character we are always limited—in appearance we may try to make ourselves look smaller or less noticeable. In action, we will not allow ourselves much scope for fear of failure or simply attracting outside attention. We feel our emotional resources are meagre and in fact they are, since our energy is constantly being scattered outward in the projection of fear.

On the evolutionary path to higher emotions, Fear is the first gate. It might block our path momentarily, but it must be gone through. Fear raises our awareness, and can be a powerful motivating force. It raises our energy to a level more capable of survival than apathy, grief and unconscious resentment. Nevertheless, fear has its pitfalls. If we run away from it, deny or suppress it, fear can rigidify our energy into the helplessness of paralysis. Once we have faced our fears and vanquished them, we can unlock the gate to a more proactive life.

Playing dead

As a primitive survival reflex, an animal that is overwhelmingly threatened by a predator will sometimes play dead, since flight will provoke the predator to chase and invariably kill it. If the animal survives, that reflex is reinforced, and it will use it again.

A person in a near-dead Apathetic Character is similar in energy to the animal 'playing dead'. Energetically it looks like the person is entranced, half asleep, or suspended in a semi-conscious state. A great many *samskaras* need to be discharged before the Apathetic Character can 'escape' into lighter energy which enables survival. Usually he simply doesn't care enough about himself to make any effort to help himself, or about life in general to want to survive. A crisis can sometimes force a change in this situation—or being apathetic can immobilise him. With the reduced awareness and low energy of apathy, he might not recognise that something disastrous is happening and fail to survive the crisis simply because he doesn't move in time.

Poor me!

Sometimes emotions are in present time and deserve our full attention. At other times they seem genuine but are simply a Character's reactive expressions. It's important to differentiate between a Grief-stricken Character, for example, and someone who has recently experienced bereavement or severe loss. The *Character* identifies with being a sad person and cannot let go or move out of his Grief. He cannot differentiate between what happened in the *past* and what is happening *now*. Often he will use his past tragedy as an excuse for not moving on. When we experience grief as a result of loss, however, it is a natural process and does not last forever, even though at times it seems there is no end in sight.

The energy of a Character in Grief is heavy, fixed and concentrated and tends to 'suck' inward. Those around him often feel drained and that they need to offer him something—such as a cup of tea, or a reassuring touch on the arm. Giving something solid and tangible is often the only way we can connect with a person in chronic Grief.

Poor you!

Similarly, the energy of a Sympathetic Character can often make others feel much worse than they did before coming into their company. Their energy is heavy, fixed and concentrated and tends to 'dump' on others, rather than drain energy from them as the Character in Grief does. Like the Rescuer, a Sympathetic Character makes people feel worse because he needs them to feel helpless so he can then offer 'help' or sympathy.

Who, me?

In contrast, the Social Butterfly Character has a light, fluid, diffuse and scattered energy. She seems literally to flit from one energy source to another, and though she never really drains other people, it is only because she spreads herself around so thinly. She seems incapable of flowing energy back in any consistent way.

Look at me!

As well as space and energy, there are several strong visual cues we can use to help identify a particular Character: their dress, deportment and bearing, and their body language.

Look around. A Character's possessions, including their clothes, are a direct indication of their self-image and their self-esteem. Dress is probably the most obvious indicator, followed closely by deportment and body language.

Clothes and lifestyle maketh the Character

Clothes can give us confidence to display ourselves or enable us to hide. It's a cultivated look, no matter how smart, scruffy, old, polished or chic. The way a Young Urban Professional dresses and the car he drives will suit his smart image, while a Dance DJ will have quite a different look. Outdoor Adventurer or Weekend Warrior Characters will go for a rugged image, a four-wheel-drive and a studied, casual look. A high school or university student who considers herself a Nerd will dress differently, with a vastly different level of confidence, to a Cheerleader Character or Sports Jock. A Student Activist Character will choose poverty, or at least the look of poverty, as a social or political statement, while Hippie Baby Boomers who marched against the Vietnam War are stolid, superannuated conservatives in the eyes of their children or grandchildren. Many empowered Characters such as Celebrity, Business Mover-and-Shaker or Sports Star define their self-image by social status, by the trendiness or opulence of their homes and possessions. They don't have to be wealthy, but usually there is more than just an eye cocked to fashion. They can more often afford to follow good nutritional diets or dietary fads than disempowered Characters. They may also choose a decadent lifestyle involving substance abuse as part of the cool image they seek.

Strike a pose

In uniform, a Nurse, Chef or Policeman Character will have a changed posture and demeanour to when in street clothes. When a Policeman's uniform includes a gun, it can give an extra swagger, power and status to the person wearing it.

A Character's bearing, way of moving and speaking all depend on how the Character feels about itself, and this can be sourced to the *samskaras* which gave the Character birth. Each Character has its own posture in which it feels comfortable, and its own habitual and unconscious body language. This may be a helpful pointer to which Character we are in at any given time.

Eleven-year-old Vince was chosen by his teacher to be the week's class monitor. Instantly he changed his posture from his usual slumped, bored manner to an erect, alert stance more befitting his new position of responsibility. He pushed his chest forward and his shoulders down and back, his chin came up and his eyes lit up, watching for opportunities to play the Class Monitor Character. During that week his usually dishevelled clothing looked neat, clean and pressed, and his hair was less unkempt. Everything in his bearing suggested reliability and competence. The following week, another child was given the position, and Vince's slackened posture indicated he felt less important as a person. Head down, his shoulders rounded and his chest concave, his contracted space showed he was back in the Character that preferred not to be noticed.

A Steamroller in power suits

Shona has a Steamroller combined with Career Woman Character who operates her high-level advertising agency in elegant power suits, expensive tailored blouses and killer stiletto heels. Her hair is always immaculate, her jewellery expensive and subtle, not flashy. She hardly seems to stay still, and when she walks it is usually at a half-run, her body held at an oblique angle, her head and shoulders leading. The Steamroller meets with quite a lot of resistance and so has gathered a large amount of force to counter it. Her muscles are held tensely ready for any argument and she runs mostly on nervous energy. The Steamroller has to get things done for a deadline so she hustles other people, galvanising them with her energy so she doesn't fall behind. Staff know to get out of her way and not to interrupt her when she is in full-steam-ahead mode, or they will be flattened into Doormats, which she does not appreciate around her. She has been known to sack a Doormat peremptorily and literally move on without missing a step.

Occasionally this Character fails totally, especially when she tries to run her relationships the way she runs her office. Needless to say the Career Woman does not have much time for relationships, but Shona is human after all and her loneliness breaks through whenever another relationship has failed. Her shoulders sink and her normally straight body curves into a shallow C, the sharp angle of the Steamroller lost in a soft surrender to gravity. Her chin is almost on her chest and her space is contracted. She is apathetic, unable to make decisions or stand up for herself. She wears soft, over-large tracksuits and t-shirts, her hair is uncombed and her face free of make-up. She can spend hours curled up on the sofa, watching old movies, eating chocolate and hugging a pillow, feeling miserable, not wanting to move. The next day at the office, the Steamroller is back, and even fiercer towards anyone exhibiting any Doormat tendencies. What she hates in herself she hates also in others and she drives herself and others harder in a futile attempt to eradicate it.

Resistance to any Character, shown in hating it, suppressing it or in pretending it is not there, simply makes it stronger, because the Character has its seed in the unconscious and this must be revealed before the Character can be deconstructed. The first step to defusing a Character is to become aware of its source and then to understand its mechanisms. Taking conscious control of the Character leads the way for the true Self to be present.

Physique—take a sneak peek

Years of training are obvious in a soldier's bearing, or a ballerina's walk, even when they are just walking the dog. In the same way, when we identify with a particular Character over a long time or in our formative years, our physique can often indicate that Character. Energy structures are more rigid, as old energy blocks, constantly reinforced, manifest in chronic physical tensions and shortened or slack muscles.

The Academic, Computer Nerd or Geek Character's posture may give the impression of no body below the neck, a bit like a tadpole. He leads with his forehead as thinking is the way in which he has survived best. So his body may be uncoordinated and move clumsily, while his intellect and his voice demonstrate certainty in his chosen field. Nevertheless, a muscle-bound body-builder can relax and soften if he takes up tai chi or growing orchids, while a sedentary academic could buff up through weight-training, should he wish. Dependent on age and health, each of these body types can reverse the trend of their physical development. Physical change usually follows the running out of a Character, but there is no reason that we can't help our Characters run out by changing our physique to something that feels more like the real, balanced us. The structure that creates a stuck Character loosens, resulting in greater flexibility in our life.

Body talk

A Character's body language is another easily observable and often tangible way to tell different Characters apart—usually in others, at first. The way a Character holds itself shows its predominant emotion.

The subtle language of physical posture comes into play whether there is verbal communication or not. Certain Characters will habitually use a particular, unconscious body language which will project their attitudes, resulting in a predictable reaction from others, either at a distance or in close proximity. Body language can betray our true thoughts whether we intend to broadcast them or not. When a fluent body reader is faced with someone who shakes their head while saying 'yes' and smiling, he can suppose some insincerity or uncertainty in the other person and expect to be let down. The man who sits with his legs and arms crossed while saying mildly 'I understand' is really saying that he is unreceptive to the ideas just outlined, though wanting to appear agreeable.

Our body language is the legacy of our pre-verbal animal forebears and of the fact that although we are spiritual beings, we inhabit an animal body. A man with his 'tail between his legs' shows the same emotions as a cowed dog: defeat, loss of face, submission to a greater force. A woman who tells a female rival to 'keep your claws off my man' indicates that she sees her as a predatory feline.

A predator—whether animal or human—will attack more readily if the prey adopts a Victim posture and/or runs, than if it can stand to defend itself. Strength in numbers is an important feature in potential victimhood or survival for both humans and animals. A Victim usually looks alone, rejected or isolated from caring family or friends. Their energy is fragile and abandoned, their space small and contracted, whereas a cared-for individual shares their space energetically with a larger group, even when they are physically alone.

Who's walking?

While knowing how our Characters walk, stand, sit and hold themselves helps identify which Character we are in, it also helps us consciously to 'flip' from a disempowered Character to the more capable opposite. Once we can identify the Character we are in, we separate ourselves from it and cease to be 'in' it simply by changing the way we stand and walk.

A Character's posture is a consequence of habitual, rigidified energy structures, and by acting from the conscious will, some of that rigidity can be dissolved. By deliberately taking over a Character's habitual physical characteristics, we literally put more of our Self into them.

Listen here

Each Character often has a recognisable tone of voice, with different elements of timbre, pitch, volume, inflection, projection, articulation, emphasis and sometimes even accent, which helps enormously with identification when working on our Characters. The chronic tone and timbre of Characters' voices are factors determined generally by their habitual thoughts and emotions. A whine or roar, a voice that 'stops at the teeth', a voice with innuendo, doubt or restraint in it, or one flat and devoid of expression, all effectively match certain Characters.

Few Professional Characters or Roles use merely the voice and attitude more effectively than the Sergeant-Major, in or out of the armed forces. The Sergeant-Major is the lynchpin of military parade grounds and simultaneously the nightmare of enlisted men. He is responsible for discipline, drills, morale, dress standards and deportment of the men, and uses his stentorian voice as a bludgeon or a crowbar as required, producing tough fighting men who can cope with any situation. Whether bellowing orders on the parade ground, blaring instructions in barracks, or inspecting the troops with blistering sarcasm, few would dare counter the Sergeant-Major or suffer his caustic verbal blitzkrieg.

At the other end of the scale, if we can recognise our Little Girl voice before the Character has gone into full swing, we can change to something more appropriate by changing the voice. A friend can often help by pointing out a 'lecturing' voice, patronising tone or a Victim's whine—although it takes great strength of character to accept these kinds of comments as 'help'!

When we first begin to work on ourselves, however, our voice is often disconnected from our emotions, and we may unconsciously communicate exactly what we do not wish to say. It is interesting that many a 'stuck' Character has repeatedly been told in their childhood to 'be quiet', to 'shut up' and generally not draw attention to themselves. Though repressed, these emotions are not entirely buried and they simmer away below the surface, only to burst out—often violently—in verbal explosions triggered unexpectedly in inappropriate situations.

In deep transpersonal healing work, it is one of the early breakthroughs when a person can allow their *samskaras* to express cathartically in the voice. It has a particular quality and literally carries the *samskara* out from unconscious to conscious expression. It is a powerful moment, a turning point in the work, when cognition can follow on cognition, and compulsive reactions can be rapidly defused.

What can I say?

Listen carefully to the words and phrases a Character uses. One of the most fundamental ways we can move beyond our Characters is to develop an awareness of how what we say reveals our limiting beliefs. Our negative thinking has attractive power enough, but words are the cement for *samskaric* structures. When we use negative words and the emotions they express, they vibrate in the larynx, causing an astral/etheric resonance that attracts other negative vibrations and thought patterns already in the environment. Self-limiting thought-forms become solidified structures when we habitually repeat a vocabulary that blocks our progress.

Phrases such as 'I can't', 'yes but', and 'if only' are common scripts for disempowered Characters—phrases which disempower them even further. Frustrated and Angry Characters frequently use phrases containing expletives. This expression of their rebellion against the restrictions in the language of polite society is a symptom of the aggravation of more personal annoyances which have set them off. Exasperated phrases in the accusative 'Why the hell don't you . . . !', 'I *expected* you to do this!', 'You always . . . !' or 'You never . . . !' lead to self-imposed perpetual frustration and the continual disappointment that goes with expectations imposed on others. Helpless Characters habitually use 'I wish . . .', 'It's so hard!', 'What's the use!' and 'It always happens to me!', generally in an apathetic tone of voice. Unconsciously Resentful Characters use 'if only' as well, dwelling on what might have been to trap themselves firmly in despair that the past and the present (and certainly the future for them too) are not as they wished, and thereby disabling themselves from doing anything to change it.

But I'm no good at that sort of thing . . .

Agnes liberally sprinkled every spoken sentence with 'I don't know', 'I mean . . .' and 'you know'. Most of her sentences ended with 'sort of thing', and would trail off uncertainly before her meaning was fully communicated. These phrases were automatic space fillers, simply intended to maintain interest in her listeners while she thought of something to say. It had the opposite effect. After a short while, most listeners would grow tired of these meaningless phrases and stop listening.

These phrases unconsciously signalled Agnes' lack of self-esteem and her uncertainty about any subject on which she was speaking. They were the main script voiced by her Dumb Character, which took over whenever she was asked to put her attention on anything out of the ordinary. The Dumb Character felt it knew nothing and was stupid, and would try to hide that with automatic filler phrases which invited—even required—others to fill in her meaning for her. When this didn't work, being the Dumb Character allowed her to hide behind a mask of stupidity, so she was not challenged to think or be insightful. The Dumb Character enabled her to be lazy.

In a Character Workshop, Agnes was banned from saying these phrases and bravely agreed to having lapses pointed out by fellow attendees. At first, she was astounded at how often and how automatically she said them. Secondly, she found she had to deal with the uncertainty these automatic phrases were designed to cover. Agnes gradually became more comfortable with uncertainty, realising it was okay not to know everything. She discovered that when she said 'I don't know', it often automatically stopped her thinking, in an anxious fog that would then become a mindless space where rationality couldn't operate. This in itself became a block to knowing. If she paused instead, and allowed the question to filter down past her Dumb Character's automatic, mindless anxieties, she could usually find an answer that expressed what she was really feeling and thinking.

It was a matter of calming herself, allowing silence, and then using language in a way that didn't cover up her supposed ignorance. It helped that at first her fellow workshop attendees gave her encouragement every time she took the time to think and feel instead of filling the silence with 'I don't know'. By the end of the workshop she found that instead of remaining Dumb, she was actually finding meaningful answers. Her Dumb Character began to break down and Agnes herself could take over.

Silencing the Inner Critic

At times we can be aware of an inner commentary of deprecating words like 'You idiot, what did you do that for? You're hopeless, what a fool!'

It's the Inner Critic Character.

When we become conscious of this voice we can stop it before it ruins our confidence completely, which happens when we mistakenly believe its negative messages. By listening carefully and sourcing these phrases we can often recognise our parents' or other authority figures' voices internalised in our thinking patterns. Sourcing a trend like this often defuses its automatic nature, and we can consciously put it back in the past where it came from. This gives a certain detachment which allows us to break the habit.

It's so much easier to do this if we can relegate those words and negative thought patterns to a Character we are aware we have, but which we also realise is *not our true Self*. We can put it in perspective. 'Oh, right,' we might say, 'that's my Punitive Saboteur Character! That's what she always says. So what.' This is an acceptance of the Character as so much background noise, and not resistance, which will only make it stronger.

It also helps to have an automatic *positive* phrase that follows and neutralises each of the Inner Critic's vitriolic comments—something along the lines of 'I love and accept myself' or 'Every day, in every way, I am letting go more and more.' Such a mantra needs to be individually right, chosen by the person because it is effective in neutralising the lacerating words of their Inner Critic. We may not fully believe we *do* love and accept ourselves, but understanding that fact is part of the willingness to create self-respect and increase self-esteem. And cultivating an automatic counter to negativity at least ensures we don't continue to erode our self-worth.

Becoming conscious of the effect of our Characters' vocabulary on ourselves and on others is a powerful step towards eliminating the compulsive element in those Characters. By identifying Characters' vocabulary and scripts we can see more clearly where they begin to take over. If we then consciously change the script to a more empowered one—of a Role, especially utilising 'I' messages—we can go a long way towards changing habitual thoughts and behaviour patterns.

When we avoid using danger-words like 'can't' and 'yes, but' and replace them with words that open possibilities instead of closing them, the energy structure of the *samskara* behind the Character is undermined, and a new, more positive structure is formed. It doesn't mean we have to go around with a Happy Face/Positive Thinker Character that sees everything optimistically—and unrealistically. It's about developing resourceful problem solving. 'I'll find a way around this' and 'yes, *and*' are handy habits to develop to break down the astral pull of our worn-out old Characters.

Speaking the Truth

Our voice is the human instrument for communication and expression, and while in animals it is a way of communicating in areas mostly relating to survival, in human beings it assumes the archetypal aspect of a potential organ of the Will and the Self. The closer we get to our divine blueprint, our Archetype, the more the voice conveys the Self and the Will connected to spiritual beings much higher in evolution than man. Ultimately the voice carries the connected Will and the connected Self so that only Truth is communicated.

7

The duality within: pairs and flips

As fascinating as it is to discover the existence of Characters in ourselves and others, it is even more interesting to observe that our Characters often come in pairs of opposites—and that, depending on our circumstances, we can actually 'flip' from one Character to its very opposite. So Party Girl out with her friends can be Melancholy Mel at home alone, and a man who is a Mouse at work could become a Tyrant at home.

An emotional see-saw

Generally, there is a weak Character and a strong Character in any given pair. If you look closely you'll notice that the pair exhibit two extremes of an energy continuum of power/no power or action/paralysis. One Character will be purposeful, the other apathetic; one creative, the other destructive. Or one will be angry, the other sad; one will lacerate herself with self-criticism and loathing while the other will have grandiose illusions of genius. In an extreme, pathological case, which is not a subject of this book, this can be a manifestation of bipolar disorder, requiring medication for extremes of mood over which the individual has little or no control.

In Characters, however, the opposites are polarities of habitual behaviour—two opposing terminals creating an energy structure by the tension between them. It's like a see-saw on a fulcrum. At the centre of the see-saw, the fulcrum is the Self, while the Characters are at either end of the plank. When we are 'in' one Character of the pair, we have only the attributes of that Character and none of its opposite's. When we 'flip', we have all the opposite attributes.

A common experience is to have an Angry Character that's powerful and intimidating, which flips almost mid-roar to a pathetic Grief Character. The impetus for the flip is often in the intensity of the emotion. Our Angry Character fumes and rages but cannot achieve any change in the situation that has triggered our anger, but which is rarely the *real* cause of our ire. Frustration sets in. We suppress the anger because we cannot deal with it, then sink into helplessness and grief. We rage until we cry, flipping to our Grief Character. The Grief Character is a Wimp, totally disempowered, and we soon get so sick of being in this Character, as do those around us, that we start to get angry again—and so the cycle repeats itself.

Interestingly this pair of flipsides is an example of both Characters being relatively powerless. There is often so much 'sound and fury, signifying nothing' in the Angry Character that nothing ever actually gets changed. All that energy is simply wasted, while the Grief Character is usually hopelessly incapable of any kind of effective action.

In contrast, when we are not in Character—not at either end of the see-saw but balanced in the centre—we can see that there are some things at which we are brilliant, others at which we are woeful and many things in between. We're human. We don't have to identify with the all-or-nothing pigeonholes of Characters. We can then consciously adopt a behaviour that is more appropriate to the situation.

A man who is a soldier, but not a Soldier/Warrior Character, can be gentle or silly with his kids, for example. He can be peaceful and creative. He can flow as spontaneously as needed, while a Soldier Character feels repelled by softness and only identifies with fighting. Similarly, a man who might flip between being an irresponsible Little Boy and a Controlling Parent might find a mature, balanced adult at the centre of the two. The adult is the *real* person, acting in present time, and not according to past conditioning.

A Happy Face flips to Old Misery-guts

Isabel was the youngest child in a family in which most of the parental attention was taken by the special needs of her disabled older brother, Nathan, who had cerebral palsy. Izzy developed a Happy Face Character to mask the deep hurt she felt at being ignored by her parents. The Character was 'born' one day when her parents were dealing with Nathan's normal demanding routine and a minor upset of Izzy's was brushed aside. Izzy decided she would never burden them with her childhood worries.

She was praised for her cheerful self-reliance, such remarks often being followed by her mother's sigh, 'Thank goodness we don't have to worry about *you*, Izzy!' The praise was a crumb. Izzy began to feel she was neither valued nor even noticed, and hated herself for the resentful, mean thoughts she harboured about Nathan.

In primary school, small personal items belonging to pupils in Izzy's class had been disappearing. To her shame, and the outrage of her parents, the missing items—along with some shoplifted trinkets and sweets—were found in Izzy's schoolbag. As Parental Persecutors, her angry parents maintained a stony lack of understanding. 'How could you do this to us? We don't have time for this rubbish. What kind of parents are people going to think we are now?' they fumed.

Izzy's parents moved her to another school. There was tacit agreement never to mention the episode again, and to disguise her deepening misery Izzy's Happy Face Character remained firmly installed for the rest of her school career. When people were fooled by her automatic act, she began to believe there was something deeply wrong with her, and that if they knew, they'd despise her and reject her. Later, as an adolescent, she despised others for being fooled. As an adult, when she had firmly identified with the Happy Face Character, she was outraged when people called her fake.

Unfortunately, people simply felt the falsity and brittle, tinsel quality of her super-positive attitude and her 'Can do!' assertions. She seemed to be gaily skating over real obstacles, ignoring them when they loomed ahead and denying them when they brought her crashing down. She simply told herself she was a Positive Thinker. Sadly, Izzy knew many people superficially, but had no close friends.

Her Happy Face Character gravitated towards an advertising career. When the first campaign for which she was responsible failed and she lost her company a great deal of money, she had a major breakdown. The flipside to her Happy Face Character emerged, and stayed for a few months. Izzy called this Character Old Misery-guts. She was too depressed to work, and was kicked out of her flat when she could no longer pay the rent. Izzy began house-sitting for people travelling overseas. She was able to utilise briefly her bright and breezy Happy Face while being interviewed by prospective employers, but later, when given the house-sitting job, she would 'empty like a balloon', and slink around barely touching anything in the house. Later, she found it ironically appropriate that she should be borrowing the homes, possessions and lives of 'legitimate' people while she was homeless. She felt like a ghost.

Through working on herself in therapy, Izzy began to realise how ingrained and fake her Happy Face Character was, and how she needed to allow time to grieve for all the things she had not allowed herself to feel as a child. She realised her childhood Kleptomaniac Character had been trying, by stealing, to provide for herself the affection of which she had been deprived. Gradually she is becoming more authentic and resilient. Izzy still sometimes defaults into her Happy Face Character, but she is able to step back, stop, and redirect herself into behaviour that is more truly her Self. Unlike the fake Happy Face Character, Isabel's own genuine warmth and brightness are lovely.

Sometimes a person exhibits only one of the pair for most of their life and maybe only once or twice in that life flips to the other Character (as Izzy did, and as Tara and Sean did in our opening example).

Genesis of two Victims

Thomas had an inveterate Victim Character, and in the process of sourcing it, recounted many years of victimisation and being bullied at school. Finally, he remembered an earlier time as a pre-schooler when he himself bullied a playmate in a remote corner of the playground, and took great glee in the feeling of power he discovered. Thomas was pulled up short by the booming voice, over the PA, of the head teacher telling him to stop immediately and report to the office. As he froze, Thomas was convinced the teacher's voice was that of God, and that he would always be seen whatever he did. He was immediately filled with shame and, during the isolation of his Time Out, vowed never to allow himself to feel that seductive power again. As he stood there miserably in the Time Out corner, four-year-old Thomas decided to be the Victim rather than the Bully, forever more. Later, whenever he was targeted he believed he deserved it.

Charlotte had a Victim Character also, but only ever remembered being teased or bullied and abused, never abusing anyone else, nor even ever standing up for herself. In fact, her sense of justice was so strong that she was embarrassed and shamed when her older brothers—whom she idolised—and their friends acted so cruelly towards her. Her early decision was never to be powerful, because all the powerful role models of her formative years were brutal and unjust.

Both Thomas and Charlotte chose to disempower themselves rather than hurt others, and through the binding *samskaric* structures of which the astral body is made, predisposed that the energy around them would be that of Victim until such time that, as adults, they could consciously change that decision.

Heroic in an emergency, a wet noodle in my life

Phoebe was first on the scene of a horrific multiple car accident. Thanks to her Rescuer Character she coped heroically until ambulance men arrived. However, later at home when there was no longer an emergency, the Character collapsed and her Helpless opposite emerged, feeling powerless and shocked and needing comforting.

For most of her life, Phoebe identified with her Helpless Character. It took an emergency to bring out her Rescuer Character, while most of the time she felt helpless, needing help herself. Once or twice she even went to the extent of unconsciously creating alarm or crises so she could swing into action. As she worked on empowering herself, she identified more with the more tonic Compulsive Helper flipside, which would bustle in with unwanted advice or practical help at every opportunity. She felt useless and hated herself whenever she was unable to help someone, or instead transferred to blaming them for being ungrateful or selfish.

What causes a flip?

A flip is determined by whether our Character is achieving the desired effect. This is usually measured in terms of how much attention, sympathy or approval the Character can win. Or it may be concerned with status, or how well it can control other people to get what it wants. So if one of the pair is failing to master the situation, we flip to the other.

A flip can also be triggered by our environment or context—the Office Mouse can flip to the Home Tyrant somewhere on the drive home. You might say the theatre and the scenery dictate the play and the Characters.

Characters seek balance and choose environments for this purpose.

What happens to the energy in a flip?

Though we can only be in one Character of a pair at one time, balance between the two is a significant factor. So when a Character has acted out to its fullest extent, a kind of tension pulls us back to the opposite. Balance is not always maintained by equal *time* spent in each Character of the pair— rather in the *intensity* of the Character's emotion.

For instance, we might *hate* being in a Victim Character, and yet find ourselves mired in this Character for weeks and months at a time. A Victim's emotions of grief and apathy and pain are extremely heavy and they literally 'suck' our physical energy. When finally the extent of that Character is reached, we might flip into Tyrant—usually coming up through anger and self-hatred. But playing a Tyrant may disgust us for *samskaric* reasons— because we ourselves have been victim to these tyrannical behaviours, and so we rapidly flip back again.

The good news is that when we flip, we can come close to the equilibrium of the true Self when we are 'between' Characters, where there is no script and we can consciously decide how we'll act. It might only be a few moments, but there is a tiny gap between the trigger and the Character reaction. Once we see the dynamics of the automatic flip to a Character, we have a chance in that short time to make a choice. When we consciously choose not to react, that time gap gets bigger each occasion and it is easier not to go into Character.

Not being in Character mode will always be a conscious choice at first, until the addictive pull of drama/melodrama, pride, punitive impulses, shame and failure is discharged, and the spontaneous freedom of the non-reactive Self becomes more comfortable.

In fact, whenever we are feeling these emotional reactions: shame, blame, regret and failure—we are absolutely in a Character, in a reaction from the past. In realising it we are detached enough to no longer be in that

Character, at least at that moment. The detachment gives us the choice to come back into the present, to not be in Character at all.

Remember, we have a choice. Observe it, but don't *blame* yourself. Choose how—and who—you want to be.

HOW DO WE FREE OURSELVES FROM OUR CHARACTERS?

There are eight steps to freeing ourselves from Characters or any unconscious behaviours. Within a therapeutic situation, discharging the *samskaras* that are at the basis of the Character's structure is enormously helpful. Outside of therapy, we can still work on ourselves, though progress will be slower. The eight steps are milestones either way. You may want to bookmark this page for future reference.

1.   The first step is *awareness* of the automatic behaviours that indicate a Character is operating.

2.   The next step is *observing* the Character's behaviour, thoughts, emotions, history, lifestyle preferences, body language, posture, preferred clothing and colours, etc.

3.   The third step is to *source* the Character. When did it arise and why? It also helps to see how the Character has operated at various stages throughout our lives, how it has been reinforced, and what choices it has made for us.

4.   Fourth, *knowing and understanding* the Character's script is crucial. In what way did the Character work once? Why does that no longer work?

5. The fifth step is to *let go of any significance* attached to the Character's existence and behaviour. No shame, blame, regret or failure.

---

6. Sixth, *know that we have a choice* to do what the Character has always done, or something different. How would *we* act, feel and be, differently to our Characters?

---

7. The seventh step involves *consciously taking the Character over.* Taking responsibility, and taking over the automaticity of the Character, means we take over its power. We can make it a Role in which we are in charge, instead of the Character being in charge.

---

8. The ultimate step is to *practise being in the present.* Since Characters act from old scripts, they are powerless when we are in the here and now. Only when we are in the present can we be in the Ego, where the observer and the observed are one in harmonious *being.*

8

Creating balance

At first, it is disturbing to discover how automatic and unconscious much of our behaviour is. When most people first encounter the notion of Characters and recognise their features in themselves, there is usually a moment of alarm when they ask, half jokingly, if they are crazy, or whether they have what used to be called Multiple Personality Disorder, now known as Dissociative Identity Disorder.

In fact, people who have multiple personalities are not crazy or insane. They are neither delusional nor out of touch with reality. One or many of the dissociated identities can function perfectly well in the world. The identities are a creative response to unbearable childhood abuses far more intense than the conditioning factors that result in Characters.

On a continuum of the mind's capacity to create personality, Characters are at one extreme, multiple personality syndrome at the other. The main differences are that before therapy, the core identity of a multiple personality is unaware of the existence of its separate and distinct personalities, and these consider themselves identities in their own right, even though they share a body. Typically, a multiple will experience gaps in time, amnesia and internal conversations, among other symptoms, and each personality will have its own memories. With Characters, on the other hand, there is no amnesia and no lost time. We can see how we are on auto-pilot in certain situations. Our Characters are not full or complete individuals, but conditioned, emotional facets of us. Our Characters do not consider themselves different people with their own names, though therapeutically it is often useful to give them a name and know that 'Barry Battler' or 'Dorothy Doormat' are only Characters and not the 'real', or whole, us. This is not dissociation but rather detachment, which allows objectivity and solution-finding.

The aim in Character work is to reach spiritual wholeness through consciously transcending reactive behaviour patterns, by taking over the automatic behaviour of our Characters. It helps to know that the single most powerful element when we start recognising some of our Characters is our *awareness* of them, while the single most limiting element is the *significance* we give them.

It is natural to develop an aversion to our Characters as we uncover them and come to understand their effect on our lives. If you can let go of any significance you give to them, you have a far better chance of mastering them than if you resist them. *Significance* is when we hate our Characters or despise and punish ourselves for having them. A better approach to take to our Characters is to realise that everyone has them.

Once we have noticed and sourced our Characters, a good line to cultivate is 'So what?' Much like rainy weather, where you would simply take an umbrella or a raincoat, don't let a bit of rain (or a Character) stop you doing what you want to do. On the other hand, don't pretend it's not really wet out there.

Taking conscious control

Becoming aware of our Characters is the first step to mastering them and reclaiming control over our lives. When we consciously observe our own automatic reactions, our awareness alters those reactions. Think of what happens when we observe the automatic process of breathing: suddenly our breathing changes. But if we *practise* breathing in a particular way, such as the *pranayama* techniques of yoga, we can consistently—and permanently—alter the length of our inhalations, retentions and exhalations. The technique has a remarkable effect on awareness and also on physical processes such as blood pressure, body temperature control and stress. Observing and practising these techniques allows control of the automatic process of breathing and expands our consciousness to cosmic proportions.

We can take over our Characters in the same way.

While a Character is a *part* of us, it is not the highest—nor even the major—part of the *real* us when we live in the present and are in control of our lives. A Character is like a fingernail caught in a car door. The pain of it takes over our awareness for some time, but ultimately it recedes. We realise we no longer need to protect the fingernail so carefully, and that there are other parts of our body that don't hurt. To believe we are our Characters is like believing we are just our injured fingernail, even after it is healed and no longer painful.

We can take responsibility for our Characters by knowing their behaviour is not consciously our present choice, and changing it.

Moving out of Victim

When I first met Jessica, she identified almost completely with her Victim Character. After being raped in her childhood, Jessica felt helpless in many situations in her adult life. At the age of 29, she was still living at home. She had never had an intimate relationship, was enmeshed with her controlling and manipulative mother and believed she could not change.

However, when we explored how she would act if someone tried to molest her now, as an adult, Jessica became fiercely angry. Her space, which she had contracted so far inside herself that no-one would be able to reach her or hurt her, began to expand and she suddenly felt more powerful than ever before. She saw she was stronger, wiser and better able to deal with such a situation than she had ever been as a child. And she had no need anymore to stay small and quiet, or be submissive to her mother. She decided the only way she could live her own life was to leave her mother's house. The part that made this decision was the real Jessica, underneath the Victim and submissive Little Girl Characters.

Jessica's changes began with an awareness that she was not being who she felt she really was underneath her external behaviour. What she had most difficulty with was the significance she put on her Characters—the inner voice that said she 'shouldn't' be in her disempowered Little Girl or Victim Characters, or that she was pathetic for being in them. When she could forgive her default into her conditioned Characters and simply accept that she was human—good at some things and needing to work on others—she made the most progress in freeing herself from their reactive pull.

Interestingly, as Jessica changed, she discovered her dominating mother was also changing, becoming more moderate and appreciative, and less controlling. Much, much later, Jessica came to the rueful conclusion that her Victim/Little Girl Character might have created—or at least contributed to—her mother's Controlling Parent Character. By that stage, however, she and her mother were interacting as adults, with mutual respect.

Using the pendulum swing

Jessica made a quantum leap when she discovered the hidden flipside to her Victim Character. At first, she was so averse to its anger that she feared even to acknowledge it. It helped her to think of Character flips as being like the swing of a pendulum.

Imagine a pendulum swinging in a doorway between a dark room and a room that is brightly lit. The pendulum can only reach as high in the light as it does in the dark. If we prevent the pendulum going into the dark, we also stop it going into the light. Preventing the pendulum from moving at all is like what happens when we get stuck in a Character. We feel dead inside. There is no life, no chance of movement, no chance of change. Using the principle of the pendulum when working with Character flips in therapy is illuminating, particularly when one of the pair is violent or cruel and we fear to let it out in case we lose control.

After many months of work, Jessica began to reclaim her belly. At first, Jessica's belly had felt energetically dead when I tuned into it—and under-standably, since her entire pelvic region had been put into trauma with the *samskara* of the rape. In time, small surges of anger indicated that her belly was becoming activated and we proceeded gently into the rage suppressed deeply within. We spent some time acclimatising Jessica to the force of anger and discharging it cathartically.

In regression sessions we can often experience the viewpoint of other people who were present in the situation, as though we are hovering above and able to dip into the thoughts and emotions of others. I asked Jessica in one session if she would go into the viewpoint of her rapist. Jessica described his attitude as all about power and domination. Her rapist had wanted to reduce her to nothing, to desecrate her and destroy her. It had nothing to do with sex and nothing to do with her personally. It had everything to do with how disempowered the rapist believed he was.

The session was the turning point in her therapy. In consciously taking the opposing viewpoint to her habitual Victim stance, something had been equalised, the balance of energy was restored, and Jessica was able to access her own anger and her own power. With her belly now alive with energy, Jessica was becoming whole once more.

The power of the pendulum analogy is that we sometimes need to experience the extreme of the dark opposite, in order to find a more balanced position that does not fear to embrace the whole.

The Suicidal Character

Teri suffered two severe depressive episodes during which she had constant thoughts of killing herself, although she never acted on these impulses. There were plenty of reasons to be sad in Teri's life, not least five deaths in her close circle. Her grandfather and her mother both committed suicide from depression. Her sister fell from a balcony while away at university and it is unclear whether it was suicide or an accident. Two friends died within months of each other, one by his own hand and one in a car accident. Apart from her grandfather, these deaths all occurred within a six-year period.

Not surprisingly, the Character's emotions were based on feeling helpless. In a regression session, Teri experienced an overwhelming helplessness and panic she had felt in the womb—an emotion that really belonged to her mother—when Teri's grandfather had committed suicide during the pregnancy. Immersed in her mother's astral/etheric bodies, Teri felt she had 'cooked' in her depression, too, but for the young girl it was the seed of an overwhelming anger.

Like her father, Teri was fiery and she fought him from an early age, while he used more and more explosive anger to cow her into submission. Teri sulked for most of her childhood and when she hit puberty acted out in a Teenage Rebel Character with wild behaviour, drugs and alcohol. Then her sister died. Teri immediately flipped to being Good, forcing her fierce anger down inside, feeling she had been wretchedly selfish. Her father withdrew, her mother became severely depressed and then suicided on the anniversary of her elder daughter's death. In her now familiar helplessness, Teri was unable to express any strong emotion for fear of what she felt were the consequences. Her own first severe depression followed.

The Suicidal Character came out of the emotional flatness she then felt, a numb space along with the sensation of heavy, painful metal plates on the top of her head that were a physical manifestation of suppressed anger. Automatic thoughts came with the mental fog to end her life so it would all be over and then people would know how she had felt. She believed she had no choice, that she was genetically programmed to kill herself and couldn't stop it. Teri felt suicide was often contagious, but then realised that because of what she'd been through when her mum died, she had no wish to inflict this on anyone else. Nevertheless, she'd wake up with suicidal thoughts which were severe until mid-afternoon. When her medication eventually began to work, the numb space, flatness and the mental fog were much less. She was at last feeling real emotions again and even though they were sad and lonely, it was better than the flatness of depression.

Though it was unbearable at the time, later it actually helped Teri that she observed her mother's depression for years, because she could see differences between them. Her mother had a strong death wish which meant she made many attempts and never sought help. Teri, on the other hand, loves this world and has long appreciated its beauty. She also has a network of support she can rely on should she need help.

She maintains she would never have actually attempted suicide, simply because she realised in time that the Character's thoughts were so childishly ridiculous and so melodramatic. She never made a plan for how she would take her life. The Character was more focused on how sorry everyone would be when she was dead.

Unlike her Suicidal Character, which desperately resisted feeling sad, Teri now allows herself to be sad when she needs to be, and it passes. It's very different to the all-encompassing bleakness of depression. She recognises the deeper empathy she now has for others' pain and the caring wisdom she has gained. She takes responsibility for keeping herself emotionally and mentally healthy by exercising regularly and working at a job she loves. In seeing the difference between her Characters' thoughts and her own, she has perspective on her life and how she wants to be.

From darkness to light

Fergus came into a session with the discovery of what he called a Day-Late-Dollar-Short Character, which could earn just enough to pay a bill but was usually late and a little short of the full amount. The Character emerged whenever he had to pay bills or ask for his fee. He described it as a Wimp Character, afraid of offending people by asking for what he was entitled to; full of fear and guilt. In this Character, Fergus felt he never had enough of anything, including air to breathe. He felt it most in his chest, like a band restricting his lungs and heart.

He had first become aware of it when he was small. He'd made a decision not to ask his single mother for what he needed or wanted, such as new shoes or a new bike, because there was never enough money to go around. This decision to do without was still operating in his adult life, a decision we later reversed in the session, and replaced with a conscious, unrestricted attitude that accepted abundance. In the meantime, he noticed how the Character affected his posture, making him hunch his shoulders to protect the part of his chest being squeezed. His neck and shoulders were chronically tight as a result.

When I asked him what the Character would be if it were an animal, Fergus was surprised to come up with an insect. It was a slater—grey, small, having no neck, and with armouring like a tiny armadillo. A real-life slater scuttles under logs and rocks, preferring dark, moist places. It's also a scavenger, living on what others leave. Fergus laughed ruefully at the image of himself as the Slater asking for his fee, and expressed no surprise that in that state he invariably got squashed.

Fergus felt the animal flipside to this Character was a Lion: huge and magnificent, the Lord of the Jungle, imperious, entitled to the best kill, the biggest pride, and the most females. He had loved lions as a boy, and in the session, he felt the energy of the Lion in his heart for the first time. It made his whole body feel strong, powerful and grounded. He felt that if he were the Lion, no-one would ignore him. In fact they'd seek him out. The Lion would be an asset to any business, effective, popular and successful, and would have no trouble asking for a fee that was his entitlement. He decided to make the Lion his business logo.

I asked him if the Lion was the real Fergus, and he paused. He said that perhaps the Lion, with its killer instinct, was a little too fierce to be him, though it felt more right than the Slater. I mentioned that since he had identified each of them, it was likely that he could access elements of each, consciously and deliberately. If he needed to impose a fierce presence on business competitors, he simply needed to practise letting himself feel the energy of the Lion. As he felt it in the session, his face glowed. Within his own heart, he told me, he felt a warm golden feeling like the sun, radiant and shining. The energy in the room grew soft and full.

For long, silent moments, Fergus basked in this golden sun, then told me he also felt strength, compassion and love, and expansive, life-giving energy. It made him feel incredibly light.

I asked him how it would feel if he had this energy in his life. Awed, he realised it made him feel there were no limits, and the feeling was so tangible, so real, and vast. This was far more than just the Character of the Lion.

Fergus had experienced his true Self, as represented by the golden sun. It's no accident that the sun is the symbol for the Self in astrology, and for Life and wholeness in many ancient traditions, or is deified. The qualities he had felt were his own true qualities—and there were more to be discovered. He decided his new business logo would not be the Lion, which he now saw as one of his Characters, but the sun, which would help him remember the fullness and completeness of his true Self.

As Fergus continued working on his Characters, his business, and his life, improved. Consciously accessing the Lion flipside helped him to realise his inherent nobility and his worthiness. Once the powerful, noble but misguided childhood decision to do without was reversed, he was free to make another decision about how he really wanted to be, in his present and future.

In his daily meditation, Fergus re-creates the feeling of the sun's presence within him, not by mental processes of imagination or creative visualisation, but by going into his heart and finding the sun already there. It is significant that this is not an imposed idea, but something he experiences as the true him. From there, he allows the sun's natural expansiveness to radiate until it fills his entire body and then his energy field, the space around his body, and eventually the whole room. This daily practice is part of a course in subtle body building through which Fergus is landing an impressive Egoic presence. The process is causing the astral structures which locked in his Characters to fall away from disuse.

SPACE EXPANSION EXERCISE
Intermediate

1. Sitting comfortably with eyes closed, place your attention on your solar plexus. Remember, no visualisation, no effort, no rush. Just allow the natural expansion of your space. Spend some time in each phase of the exercise. Move on to the next stage when you have managed the one you are in.

   ———————————

2. Do the expansion exercise as you've practised (see Chapter 6), to fill the room with your presence.

   ———————————

3. With eyes open or closed, while sitting very still, allow your space to expand to include the whole building you are in.

   ———————————

4. Become aware of the street, and expand your space to include the street and all the buildings along it. You might become aware of your neighbours, animals, delivery people, pedestrian and road traffic.

   ———————————

5. Expand your space around your entire suburb or local area. Become aware of schools, hospitals and shops and the people using them.

   ———————————

6. Expand your space over your entire city or town. Remember you're still in your body, sitting in your room, while your awareness is spread, allowing you to sense-know the energy of your city or town, and how it is different in some areas.

   ———————————

7. In stages, see how far you can expand your space. Can you expand over your whole state or country? Can you expand your space over the hemisphere you live in, or the entire globe? Can you expand to include the moon's orbit? At each stage, sense-

feel the differences: the northern hemisphere compared to the southern, various states, countries and cities compared with each other. What does the moon feel like compared to the earth? Note if at any time you feel uncomfortable or if it ceases to be an experiential expansion exercise and becomes mere visualisation. In this case, gently go back to where you last *felt* the expansion.

8. When you have expanded as far as you feel comfortable, come back in slow stages, sensing once again the differences in energy as you contract your awareness back to your city, suburb, street, building and room. With practice you can become remarkably accurate in differentiating the energy of different places and you will experience expansion of your own personal space with increased comfort.

9

Two to tango . . .

In relationships of many kinds we can often find ourselves in the same kind of dynamic as a Character pair, where one of us is in a powerful Character and the other is disempowered.

In marital relationships, there are still couples who have accepted the traditional power roles of dominant male and submissive female, in Characters that match. There is a certain stability to these hierarchical roles, to the point that some people believe a stable society depends on maintaining them.

In traditional gender roles, men often find the burden of being strong and unemotional unbearable, while sacrificing close relationships with their children. Women can give up their independence and often their self-esteem by taking on a role which relegates them to the kitchen and caring for family, if this is valued less than going out to work. Both sexes sacrifice personal growth in areas the other sex has traditionally filled. This is more obvious today than ever, when outwardly it seems equality is possible between the sexes, at least in the West.

There are changes. Home dads and house-husbands are increasing, especially when paid work can be done online from home, adding to the usual home-office businesses such as book-keepers, architects and artists. Couples are coping with changing status issues when traditional roles are reversed, and yet few would claim that this added complexity makes them happier. When things get more complicated, we frequently cope by sliding into other stereotypical Characters.

The hard-won battles of feminism against a patriarchal meme seem to have achieved much less than was hoped. Equal work still does not attract equal pay across the board. In companies citing economic rationalism rather than human values or quality of personnel, a man will still be hired in preference to a woman who might start child-bearing or who already has the lion's share of child-rearing responsibilities. There are certain industries that are exceptions, such as publishing, where 95 per cent of the staff are women, but there are enough male-dominated business arenas for it still to be newsworthy when a woman makes it to the upper echelons. A woman in power is still often criticised for her weight, her dress sense or for being a 'Dragon Lady' rather than praised for her policies or achievements.

On the other hand, a woman who chooses to stay at home and look after her children is often patronised. As a result, many women model themselves on a Superwoman Character—attempting to balance the demands of home and family responsibilities as well as career advancement. Meanwhile, younger women seem to model themselves on the Pussycat Dolls or Britney Spears. The rampant sexualisation of music videos means that sexual role models dominate over more balanced personality development from an earlier age than ever before. Naturally Characters proliferate here.

Despite the social and sexual freedom of modern young women in the West, it seems Generation Y not only takes for granted the advances so painfully won by their feminist older sisters, they appear not to value them at all—perhaps because they no longer feel they have to fight for equal rights. It's interesting that few young women these days have their mothers' determination to fly in the face of gender stereotypes: the Characters of Teen Sweetheart, Blonde Bimbo and Barbie Doll seem only slightly diluted versions of the more mature Porn Queen and Sex-Bomb Characters. They are, however, forgoing their personal identity just as sacrificially as the housebound Wife-on-a-child-bearing-conveyor-belt, albeit with an apparent boundless sexual freedom.

To match them, Characters such as Party Boy and Stud, and younger versions Studmuffin and Spunk, are their partners in the developmental phase of sowing wild oats and playing the field. It's a phase which also seems to be lasting longer than in previous generations. Such stereotypes cannot create loving relationships to which each partner might bring the fullness of their whole being.

We have to be a real person, first.

You're becoming your mother!

In relationships, both women and men find it difficult to escape the Character modelling of their parents. Sometimes we go to the opposite extreme—as conservative adult children of ageing Wild-Child Hippies demonstrate. However, often it's something we only notice in our relationships or when we become parents, when we find we are playing out exactly the same kinds of scenarios we hated in our parents. What we resist, persists.

Consciously we may both be aiming for the ideal of equality. Or we may be jockeying for the more powerful position in the pair. Since nothing is static, relationships included, the flips that then sometimes occur are interesting. The couple begins to operate as though they are on the Character pair see-saw, with one being up while the other is down, and then they swap. It is impossible for a couple playing this sort of unconscious game to ever be equally empowered—at least at the same time.

Sometimes in the dynamics of Character flips there is no tacit agreement for one partner to be up while the other is down. As soon as one goes down in energy or status, the other is unconsciously jealous of the attention thus gathered and goes down too, competing for sympathy. The first one to fail to get sympathy will bounce up again in an effort to get attention for being in control, and can be scathing in their lack of sympathy for their partner. The partner then flips up to compete once again for Top Dog.

Hot screen, cold sheets

Sex in relationships is often the area where Characters, rather than the true Self, are in complete control. Often when one partner is needier, or wanting more sex, the other becomes distant. The more unobtainable one partner is, the more the other is in pursuit. A chases B, then B turns suddenly to chase A, only to find A rapidly retreating, as with Chloe and James.

Chloe and James have been married for six years and have a three-year-old son, Josh. Their sexual relationship had petered out since Josh's birth, though Chloe said it had never matched her early hopes. James had a Workaholic Character, and increasingly it appeared he had lost interest in sex. Chloe, in the meantime, had developed a Yummy Mummy Character who drew admiring glances at the gym, yoga class and supermarket, and a few propositions which she declined, amused and flattered. It seemed the only one who wasn't noticing her was James. The more Chloe tried to turn James on with lingerie or arranging baby-free nights so they could have candle-lit dinners, the more distant and irritable James became. Chloe was hurt and increasingly suspicious that James was having an affair. The situation only worsened when James' work contract was not renewed and he started working from home as an online consultant. Chloe hoped that increased proximity would mean they would get closer emotionally, or at least that they could share child-care, giving Chloe more freedom, perhaps to find a part-time job. Instead, James shut himself in his home office and shouted angrily whenever he was interrupted.

Chloe got sneaky and installed a key-logger on James' computer. She was shocked to find that James was spending hours in porn chatrooms and live-cam websites. Far from having an affair, he was distancing himself even more from intimacy and opting for the instant stress relief that anonymous porn offered. It was at the stage of an addiction, and James hadn't worked in weeks.

Chloe confronted him and he was indignant, maintaining that it was normal and healthy. She dragged him to couple counselling, but he bailed at the last moment. Chloe started a part-time job to help their ailing finances. With her attention diverted, there were some stagnant months. There were several teary attempts to communicate how disappointed and upset she was, as well as efforts to get him to tell her how he was feeling. It would have been easier to milk butterflies. Chloe gave up and decided to find someone who was more emotionally accessible and sexually compatible. She took their son with her to stay in a friend's flat while the friend was overseas.

As soon as she left, James realised his life was empty without her and Josh. In his Ardent Lover Character, he sent her flowers, emails and a barrage of text messages. He rang several times a day. He apologised and said he had changed. He missed her desperately and couldn't understand how he'd been so stupid. However, when she said she would come back only if he attended counselling for his porn addiction, he became silent. He saw her then as Ice Queen, imperious and implacable.

Chloe remembered how he had been so persistent in pursuit when they'd first met, while she had then been cool about him. Once married, she remembered how he had justified longer and longer hours at work, away from the relationship. She came to the conclusion that she knew him very little, and he knew himself even less. She realised that she had exhausted all her affection for him as well as her tolerance. James was heartbroken, but Chloe was gone.

Fear of intimacy

The Pursuer–Pursued Character Game often flags fear of intimacy in one or both people. James was afraid of what Chloe would think of him when she found out who he was deep down. Chloe on the other hand had initially been afraid that intimacy with James would mean she would be submerged, that her life would be taken over by his. Now, Chloe understands that intimacy means holding on to ourselves while we open to the gaze of someone whose opinion is very important to us. If our partner's view of us holds more weight to us than our own, we will avoid intimacy. We will avoid showing our deeper selves, our desires and fears, in case of rejection. As a result, our relationship will not grow. It won't remain exciting and fulfilling. It will stagnate and eventually die.

To counter the fear of disapproval we all feel to some degree, we need to develop the ability to self-soothe. We need to make our own opinion of ourselves more important *to us* than anyone else's. It means we remain self-determined rather than dependent on the opinions of others for how we feel about ourselves. It's the challenge of being adult in a relationship, detailed by Dr David Schnarch in his book *Passionate Marriage*. If we can present ourselves to our partner with trust, without anything held back, we invite the same courage and commitment in our partner. If we can soothe ourselves when we fear rejection, or even when we are in fact rejected, we can stop hiding and be ourselves in the relationship.

Fear of sex

Jo was an attractive young woman who received frequent, unwanted attention from men. Molested by her stepfather, she felt she was frigid and too inhibited ever to enjoy normal communication with men, let alone sex. Her upbringing had been restrictive, somewhat puritanical and replete with parental double standards. At the age of fourteen her mother had told her that she was cheap and that boys would only ever want her for one thing. At this time, due to her early abuse, she was herself sexually molesting her younger siblings in an imitative way.

When she was eighteen her first date shocked her by pushing his advances on her, saying she had 'asked for it'. Similar date-rapes followed. She began to work with me to examine her suspicion that she was somehow drawing the situation on herself. Her deeper guilt towards her siblings emerged much later.

Jo felt dirty and sexually degraded as a result of her stepfather's molestation, and through guilt at what she had done to her brother and sister. She was sure people could see what she was, despite the concealing clothing she habitually wore. The more she consciously resisted her inner identification with a Promiscuous Character, the more it stuck in her mind, and she discovered that in this way she had been unconsciously projecting herself as sexual prey. The flipside was a fearful Prude Character. Both Characters gave an inordinate amount of attention to sexuality, one hyper-aware of her sexual attractiveness and power, the other repressing and denying any sexual impulse. She had developed the Prude to protect her siblings, and anyone else, from her own Sexual Predator, but also to avoid sexual attention from others.

With Jo I used the ISIS one-on-one regression technique to defuse her victimhood over a period of a few months. Then, in dramatic role-play within the safety of a Character class, Jo gradually became aware of the posture and body language of her Characters. She discovered that her Prude Character's fearful shoulder-hunching and quick sideways looks, coupled with hands nervously holding her elbows, actually drew out the wish to dominate and degrade in a Macho Male Character played by another class member.

After some weeks Jo shyly began to experiment with freer body language. She learned how to flirt consciously, relaxing her stance, languidly curling her hair between her fingers, and alternately tossing her head back and lowering her head and eyelashes. Initially she scared herself with the power of her new Flirt Character, because it blatantly offered an invitation to the male Character but also challenged his power.

Jo practised both her Characters until she was sure of what signals she was actually giving. Once under her conscious control, the signals were no longer compulsive. She practised saying no without getting hysterical, and yes without feeling guilty. Her new control, and a necessary self-forgiveness, allowed her to feel confident that she would never molest anyone ever again.

Suffocating those we love

Charles had an Over-protective Character which evolved out of a bullied childhood Victim, empowering himself by protecting others. Joining the police force, he took the motto 'Protect and Serve' to conscientious extremes. It was in his personal life, however, that the Character met most opposition, in particular with his two teenage daughters, whose lives he attempted to control. Safety was always his primary concern but the girls felt stifled and imprisoned.

All his married life he had imagined the worst—which to him was any pain or distress his family might suffer—and had actively tried to prevent it by restricting their freedom, simultaneously preventing their growth. His inability to confront and deal with the trauma of his own childhood was projected onto those he loved, and the thought of their suffering in any way was unbearable.

Charles' world collapsed one day when without a word the two girls left home forever. He was forced to confront the fact that he'd in fact multiplied whatever danger they may be in by never allowing them to learn how to fend for themselves, to solve problems themselves, or find out who they could trust and who they should not. At this realisation, his Over-protector jumped in to shield him and he retreated into denial, accusing his wife of letting the girls have too much freedom. Soon she, too, left him. Charles' Over-protective Character devolved into a bitter Angry Avenger, and eventually he lost his job with the police force after killing an unarmed suspected paedophile. Some short months after, he died of an aggressive cancer, not having seen his family in years.

When love turns deadly

Every now and then we hear news reports of battered wives murdering their husbands after putting up, apparently uncomplainingly, with years of abuse. Although courts and police recognise 'battered wife syndrome' and 'learned helplessness' and take such mitigating circumstances into account, invariably there are mystified comments from the community at large that the wife 'could have just walked away', instead of killing her abuser and ending up in jail.

Such comments do not take into account the powerful dynamic of Abuser and Victim in situations of domestic violence. Not only does the Victim feel utterly powerless to do anything to save herself, the Abuser Character feels unable to stop his brutal behaviour. Frequently the Abuser will feel *he* is the Victim and project his frustration onto the Victim, saying she 'made him do it'. Often she excuses him and protects him, feeling that only she understands his true nature and the pressures he is under, so colluding in her own abuse.

The helplessness both feel is real. It is the helplessness of people who have identified so strongly with their Characters that they are controlled by the reactive emotions and thoughts of those Characters.

To the Victim, both the problem as a whole and the power wielded by the Abuser are overwhelmingly enormous. A simple solution such as walking away seems impossible. Often the Victim is convinced the Abuser will find her and bring her back—and this may be the case because the Abuser needs the Victim as much as the reverse in this co-dependent relationship. Another reason is often the uncertainty of her future if she walks away: the fear this engenders may be bigger than the familiar and predictable fear she feels in her relationship. 'Walking away' is seen as less definite—or permanent—an action than murder. Nor does 'walking away' give her an opportunity to show how she really feels.

To the severely oppressed Victim, only the most extreme and permanent of solutions seems viable. She believes she *has* to kill him, and may even provoke him to further extremes of cruelty to gear herself up for an extreme reaction. Or she will only rise to action as Rescuer or Avenger when her children are threatened, giving herself permission to be violent that she cannot access as Victim. It's a matter of balancing perceived power with power of an equal magnitude.

One-upmanship at work

The same underlying dynamic is occurring when we hear, increasingly frequently these days, reports of a victimised, disgruntled employee or bullied high school student who acquires an automatic firearm and tragically turns it on his former workmates or innocent fellow students. Victims of bullying who turn homicidal feel the need to take back and assume the enormous and violent power they have projected onto their Abusers.

Cases of extreme violence aside, however, the game of opposite Characters is common in work relationships too. When a person is strongly in one Character, the tendency is for someone else in their vicinity to assume the opposite terminal. So the Tyrant Boss creates Victims in his or her staff, while a Manager or Boss Character will often manufacture or exploit competitiveness within his staff for higher productivity, leading to rivalry, jealousy and approval-seeking, with staff jockeying for prominence. Obsequious staff members will become Brown-nosers or Pleasers, while a more calculating and less covertly ambitious Character can divert peer rivals from noticing surreptitious corporate ladder-climbing by becoming the Office Flirt. The latter flips to a bright Protégé Character whenever they are in the company of an Indulgent or Paternal Boss. A Chaos Merchant can be either a boss or a subordinate—his main agenda being to stir up, covertly, some kind of hornets' nest, on which he then descends to sort out the problem and take credit for restoring order. Keeping people in ignorance of his subversive role is what this Character enjoys and he manipulates everyone, whether naive or experienced, privately giving himself the most kudos for successfully blind-siding the latter. And so it goes.

Remember that we can always be manipulated into flipping Characters as long as we are other-determined instead of Self-determined, and as long as we are unaware—particularly if we are in the presence of someone who knows which buttons to press. The more we can be conscious of who we are *not*, the closer we are to living our own lives. When we know we are not our Characters, we can avoid being manipulated by someone else, or being hijacked by our own reactive emotions.

10

A vicious triangle

Dad comes home from a hard day's work to find his teenage son oblivious and playing with the Xbox in the living room. Suddenly furious, Dad starts yelling at his son. How come he hasn't found a job yet? Does he expect his parents to provide for him forever while he bludges his life away as a couch potato? Dad pushes his son, grabs the Xbox controller, and throws it violently across the room. Dad has taken on the Character of Persecutor.

The son is shocked at the sudden violence and cowers at first in fear, trying to explain that he only just started playing a minute ago. He's taken on the part of Victim.

Mum comes in from the kitchen, startled by the noise of Dad yelling. Seeing her husband standing over her son, she begins to placate the older man while getting physically between the two males. Raising her voice to be heard, she tells her husband to give their son a break. He's been trying for jobs all week and all today. He only just came home and he's stressed and tired. He deserves his rest. Mum has become the classic Rescuer.

Dad vents his anger a bit more, saying he does his best to make his son independent and self-sufficient, but she constantly undermines him and is turning the son into a sissy and no-hoper. Mum is implacable in her son's defence. Dad starts to feel cornered. Frustrated and feeling betrayed, he starts to whine. What about *him?* He's been working hard all day—as he's done for the boy's whole life—to put food on the table and provide for all of them. No-one's ever on *his* side. No-one appreciates what he does. Everyone just takes advantage of his good nature.

Dad has slipped over into Victim, while Mum is now the Persecutor telling Dad he's an ignorant, self-centred bully with no consideration for what other people do in the family.

The son is still a little shocked, but leaps up, yelling at Mum that he doesn't need her to stand up for him, that he can do that himself. Then he rallies to his dad's defence, adding that Dad *does* work hard and reassuring him that he *does* appreciate everything he does for him. Son is now Rescuer.

Mum is furious that he rejected her help, and at his betrayal when she was defending him. Now she feels ganged up on by the apparent alliance of the two males. A momentary pause allows the son to start attacking her with accusations that *she* doesn't appreciate what his father does, she's always criticising his father and so on. Son is now Persecutor and Mum is now Victim. Dad can now take the position of Rescuer . . . and the reactive Character Game goes on indefinitely.

You may have seen a similar scenario to the above playing in a living room near you. It's an example of the Karpman Drama Triangle of behaviour, formulated by Transactional Analysis Therapist Stephen B. Karpman MD in 1968.

The Karpman Drama Triangle

PERSECUTOR
anger, criticism, blame, violence

RESCUER
compulsive help, sympathy, excuses, suppressive, gives what s/he needs, powerful only in defence of others

Reproduced by permission of S.B. Karpman, MD © 1968 by the Transactional Analysis Bulletin

VICTIM
helplessness, powerlessness, uses manipulation to control, drains energy

We can see the Triad of Persecutor, Rescuer and Victim everywhere, when we start to look. They're easy to recognise because each uses an automatic mode of set behaviours, body language, scripts and emotionally manipulative ploys which are designed to perpetuate a game. They can manifest in a family or in any group of people who spend time together, at work or in recreational pursuits. They can also emerge within ourselves as we flip between disempowerment, self-criticism and excuses.

People trapped in the Drama Triangle usually play one Character more than another. Frequently, however, they switch rapidly and resettle. Each Character is convinced the emotions they are acting out are sincere and they are offended if anyone accuses them of being in a Character. A characteristic is to blame the others in the game for provoking them rather than taking responsibility for their reactivity. Their spoken expression usually begins with the accusative 'You always . . .', 'You never . . .', in generalisations that are often hard to pin down to specific situations and that are difficult to address.

In Character workshops when we play out these triangles in improvisation, participants emerge laughing and shocked. They can so easily switch from one Character to another. Or they're dismayed that they find it so difficult to do one of the three. Generally they're stunned that it's so easy to manipulate others by guilt or blame. It's so easy to believe one's own Victim, Persecutor or Rescuer even while playing it.

A Game two can play

The same scenario can involve just two people, though the three roles are the same. Daria and Simone grew up in the same dysfunctional family and are now in their thirties. Whenever Daria talks to her sister, she brings up the subject of Simone's unmarried state. Daria launches into how Simone should live her life, ignoring the fact that her own marriage and life in general are barely functional.

Daria is a Rescuer and a Caretaker. She allows her needs to be subservient to those of others. Daria focuses on the one thing Simone does not have, trying to make her sister feel like a Victim, perpetuating a childhood pattern that allows Daria to feel superior. It is her horror of being disempowered and weak that makes Daria compulsively want to meddle in other people's lives. Only by taking the role of Rescuer and Fixer does she feel better off than the people she thinks need her help. She despises and pities people who are worse off than she is, though she constantly gravitates to them and takes false pride in believing she never needs help herself. Focusing on the needs of others means that she never has to confront her own ignored needs, which get progressively worse while she despairs that others suffer so. The 'help' and advice Daria offers are rarely what the other person can use and often what she herself needs. When they reject her help she feels she herself has been rejected.

Simone has been working on herself to rid herself of the Victim Character and to detach from the Character Games that go on in her whole family. When Simone refuses Daria's unwanted advice, Daria becomes furious and turns into Persecutor, accusing her of being arrogant and ungrateful. When Simone still doesn't buy it, Daria collapses into Victim, accusing Simone of wanting to see her miserable. Later she will need to find someone else to rescue to regain her illusory self-esteem.

Simone still reels whenever she and Daria tangle in this way. Inside, all the old triggers are still working, her childhood conditioning urging her to buy into her sister's unconscious Game and become someone who needs Daria's 'help'. After this kind of interaction, and though she fights it, Simone still habitually goes into guilt, berating herself that she is a bad person, unkind to her sister. Her own internal Persecutor arises, although it took her some time to understand why. There had always been a tacit agreement that she be the Scapegoat in the family, keeping everyone happy—or at least contributing to that illusion. Not playing Victim to her sister's Rescuer meant she was not keeping that old agreement, and that made her feel guilty.

Meanwhile, another part of Simone goes into Victim, feeling overwhelmed and hopeless and hating herself. Then her internal Rescuer will attempt to rationalise and make excuses for her. Simone feels wretched during and after these episodes, and understandably. She is a walking internal war zone until she can detach from all the reactive emotions she is feeling, calm down and let them go.

How Victims create Rescuers

Showing the power of a Victim to create Rescuers is the story of Marla and Karla. Now 50, Marla was a dancer and cabaret singer who emigrated from a turbulent, war-prone country when she was nineteen. She created a gypsy stage persona which danced the struggle and displacement of war and hopeless yearning for love. Her plaintive songs were husky with struggle, oppression and loss. No longer able to support herself this way, she also teaches dance to children.

Marla became pregnant following a one-night stand and brought up her daughter Karla, now 30, more or less on her own. Karla is also a performer, though her style is very different to her mother's, preferring singing to dance. From her first independent forays onto the stage, Karla's extraordinary voice and her exotic, beautiful face gained her immediate recognition, and after much hard work she has become successful in her own right.

Marla says she is proud of her daughter, but more often she openly resents what she sees as Karla's easy success and amazing good fortune. She has lengthy phone conversations with Karla where the only topic is herself and her struggles with her waning career, her health and her precarious financial situation. With her own friends, she goes into Martyr, complaining about the difficulty she had in bringing up her daughter alone, with no help, always giving her daughter the best so she could succeed where Marla herself has not.

Playing Victim, she manipulates Karla into helping her financially. She moans that she needs her daughter near her and that her life is even more of a struggle now Karla is overseas so much. Karla once paid for Marla to visit her overseas and put her up in a five-star hotel near where she was performing. Mysteriously, Marla fell sick every night and couldn't attend any of the performances, though during the day, sightseeing and shopping—with Karla's credit card—she made sure everyone she met knew who her daughter was and how awful it was to be so far away from her while her daughter pursued her career. Everyone was most sympathetic and Marla would return, glowing, to the hotel.

Karla feels compelled to help her mother. She allows herself to be made to feel guilty for not doing more, even though she often feels nothing would ever be enough. Karla would dearly love to talk over some of her own stresses and challenges with her mother, to get some maternal or even professional advice from Marla's experience. But if ever Karla starts to talk about her own life, Marla interrupts with something that has happened in her own circle.

On rare occasions, Karla gets angry with her mother. Then Marla cries and pulls the guilt card, which soon has Karla apologising. Karla's way of dealing with her mother's childish demands has been to keep constantly busy, and to keep geographically as far away as possible.

In other words, she's not really dealing with the situation, just avoiding it. And perpetuating it.

A Rescuer spits the dummy

Susanna's story shows a Victim turning into a Persecutor, creating other Victims, while a Rescuer learns the hard way that enough is enough.

A widow and grandma to two beautiful kids, Susanna loved to offer her time as a babysitter. When both her son Dean and daughter-in-law Cheryl were made redundant from the cannery in the rural town where they all lived, Susanna's Rescuer Character immediately offered her total support. Since Dean and Cheryl were no longer able to afford their rent, she insisted they take over her modest house rent-free, while she lived in the old mobile home parked at the side of the house. It was meant to be temporary, but weeks turned into months and then a year, and there were apparently no jobs available. The young couple claimed the dole.

Susanna had often heard the couple shouting at each other. She'd also frequently seen bruises on the children. One day she found Cheryl hitting Dean and screaming at him, while the children huddled in a corner in tears. Thereafter, Cheryl insisted that Susanna knock at the back door before coming in to use the bathroom, or cook for the kids. When Susanna was given the opportunity to double her hours at the local café where she worked, she took it. It meant she was unable to babysit as often, but she reasoned that she needed more money to help support them all and that her daughter-in-law was free to look after the kids. In reality, she was finding it hard to bear the constant tension in the house.

One night Susanna came home, looking forward to a hot bath. To her surprise the house was in darkness, her car was gone from the driveway, and her key no longer fitted the lock. Much later that night, Cheryl came home with the kids asleep in the back of the car. Susanna came out of the trailer to ask what was going on. Cheryl refused to explain, erupting instead into furious accusations that Susanna had been abusing her kids and that she'd changed the locks so Susanna wouldn't be able to get to them or snoop around. She wouldn't say where she'd been, refused to return

Susanna's car keys, and ended their conversation with a rude gesture in her mother-in-law's face.

Susanna was devastated. She waited for her son to come home that night, but he hadn't appeared by the time she had to go to work the next day. She found out from a neighbour that Dean had gone looking for work in another town. Susanna went to work every day that week as usual but was not her usual chatty self. Her son didn't come home until the weekend, when he returned from a job he'd found in a town three hours' drive away. He was astonished that Cheryl hadn't told his mother where he was.

By chance, Susanna found out from a customer at the café that Cheryl was working as a barmaid at a topless bar just outside town. Apparently Cheryl had been working there three nights a week for nearly a year without telling her husband or the dole office. Dean and Susanna had thought that she'd been visiting her own mother in a nursing home or out with friends. When Susanna was no longer able to babysit, Cheryl had increased her shifts at the bar, packed the kids with sleeping bags into Susanna's car and left them sleeping in the hotel carpark.

Resenting being a Victim dependent on her mother-in-law, Cheryl had flipped into Persecutor, taking her frustration out in physical violence on Dean and the kids. Denying her own abusiveness, she had projected her guilt onto her mother-in-law, allowing her to feel justified in locking Susanna out of her own house. She blamed her mother-in-law too when Dean had to go to another town for work. Her anger was the misdirected fury of a Victim fighting to remain helpless, while attempting to become more powerful as a Persecutor by turning Susanna into a Victim.

Finally, Susanna the Rescuer saw how easily manipulated she had been by the guilt and sympathy Cheryl made her feel. Regretfully, she asked them to leave her house. Concerned about the children, she rang Community Services. Two hours after the social worker came to investigate, Cheryl left with the kids in a hired van full of their belongings and some of Susanna's furniture, including her television.

To Susanna's immense sorrow, she has not seen Dean or her grandchildren since. The lessons she learned about her Rescuer Character came too late to salvage the relationship with her son or Cheryl, who swore Susanna will never see her grandkids again.

Stop the Game, I want to get off!

All three of these Characters have the power to step out of the Game, but paradoxically the most powerful—in terms of their ability to change the triangular drama—is the Victim. Both Persecutor and Rescuer are defined in relation to the Victim. If the Persecutor stops playing, the Victim and the Rescuer can continue on their own. If the Rescuer stops playing, the Victim and the Persecutor can keep the Game going. But if the Victim refuses to be a Victim, neither Rescuer nor Persecutor can continue in that particular Game. Of course, they may turn on each other, one making the other a new Victim in a new Game.

The Victim controls the Game by covertly generating and manipulating the reactions of the others, however 'helpless' she may seem to everyone around her.

A Victim turns Persecutor

Tessa was struggling with her Victim Character. A student and part-time sales assistant, she often found her Victim Character invited rudeness and intimidation from impatient, demanding customers. It was not a job she saw herself doing and she couldn't relate to other staff, whom she saw as superficial and catty. Isolated, the Victim felt sorry for herself. It made her feel even more pathetic, which made her even more of a target, not only with customers but with other staff.

The Victim would often flip to Unappreciated Genius, critically judging others to give herself a false sense of superiority. Tessa was working on this by turning her acute perception away from herself. She began to realise how this 'demeaning' job was actually enabling her to learn how she really wanted to be, and was a steep learning curve in assertiveness.

During the hectic holiday sale season, an impatient man made loud criticisms while Tessa was struggling with the cash register. Other customers in the queue behind him joined in. Tessa's impulse was to do what she usually did in the face of conflict—run away crying. This time she didn't, though she felt the usual surge of nausea in her stomach pushing energy up into her head, overwhelming her. She stood her ground and became aware of her belly to counter the headiness. Once in her belly, she flipped from fear to anger and served the man and the others stony-faced, using a lot of force to swipe cards and close the register drawer. She contained her anger until a granny near the end of the queue came up. Handing over her parcel, Tessa shot her a look loaded with venom, which emptied her of rage. The older woman looked down and said nothing as she shuffled away. The next customer received a bright smile, and Tessa was proud that she had managed to handle the situation without a trace of her usual Victim.

She hadn't noticed that she'd slipped into Persecutor—not with the man whose aggression she could only match silently, but with the granny. She reasoned that the granny would not have made any complaints had she not been following the man's lead, and deserved the venomous look 'because she knew better'.

Since Tessa hadn't noticed how she'd gone into Persecutor before she regained professional calm, her Higher Self had to teach her the lesson karmically. It happened within a day. She and her mother were shopping at another store where the shop assistant was busy with something. Ignoring Tessa, she eventually asked her mother if she could help her. Tessa immediately took it as a slight, and muttered under her breath, 'Looks like I'm not worth serving!' The assistant shot Tessa a filthy look. Tessa knew exactly what was behind that look—it was exactly what she'd done to the granny.

I asked Tessa how it felt to receive the shop assistant's filthy look and she was indignant: it had felt awful and she knew she didn't deserve it—unlike both the rude man and the granny, in her opinion. Yet the fact that only one of them had received it showed Tessa instinctively knew she could only intimidate the granny because a Persecutor only attacks the weak. When she came out of Victim she was really only intending to stand up for herself. She went too far and slipped briefly into the Persecutor's desire to retaliate and punish.

Tessa realised that even hateful thoughts have the power to hurt, and asked how she could be powerful without being a Persecutor.

Between the Victim's desire to run away and the Persecutor's misdirected rage, Tessa had experienced just a moment of calm strength and professional purpose, when she was handling the situation. After she had offloaded onto the granny, she regained that calm once more.

With practice, particularly if we offload reactive anger responsibly and away from the provoking situation, these short moments between Characters can be extended. Consciousness takes over from reactive behaviour. Our lives are more under our control instead of at the mercy of fiery reactions.

Tessa was still resentful, feeling that she'd been a Victim forever. Her Persecutor Character was so new to her, it wanted to punish people for the way she'd let them treat her for years. The Persecutor's strength was intoxicating and addictive, even though it scared her.

Nevertheless, however briefly, Tessa had experienced her real Self—the part that had no need to punish others nor be a Victim. She could be in control, not compulsively or reactively, but responsibly.

With practice, it could become permanent. That tiny space between the provocation and her normal reaction would grow to allow her the presence of mind to choose how to behave, from the true Self, all the time.

PROCESSING ANGER

When a Victim first starts to experience the power of anger in the belly, its seductive pull is intoxicating. It can become frightening in intensity, yet it feels so good and so powerful to express it that we might feel justified in indulging in a Persecutor Character. Because anger is such a volatile energy and there are so few occasions where it is okay to express it, we need to handle our anger safely without further suppression. We *do* need to offload it. The problem is where and how we do that.

Some therapies might recommend the expression of justified anger at an appropriate target—an abuser or dominating parent, sibling, partner or boss. In my experience, this is rarely advisable or effective until some or all of the more explosive, suppressed anger has been defused first in a safe space away from the triggering situation. It's too easy otherwise for matters to escalate out of control—and we know this or we wouldn't fear it. Once defused, talking in a rational manner about how angry we were in a specific time and situation is acceptable communication allowing possible changes in the future. Please note that this is only possible if the other person is receptive and not being defensive in reaction. Apart from that, while our anger is still undefused, unconscious acting out is almost inevitable, as well as incendiary, leading to further misunderstandings and alienation.

All our conditioning is *not* to express anger at all. When we overcome our first reluctance to go against these early prohibitions, we can find ourselves indulging in self-righteous rage at soft targets, which often incurs a stinging backlash of self-loathing afterwards. Later, when we're able to let go of self-judgment, the physical expression of anger becomes enjoyable. A great deal of cathartic anger release might need to be done before power can be safely—that is, non-reactively—handled. It doesn't have to be excessively physical, with a lot of screaming, bag-punching or pillow-bashing, although there is a time when this is powerfully effective as well as necessary, simply to feel the force of what we have formerly directed against ourselves while it was suppressed.

When I was practising martial arts, all exponents at our *dojo* knew that the safest people to spar with were the black belts, while the *kyu* grades, the beginners, were the most dangerous. The *dans* (the black belts), knew their power and were disciplined through long practice only to use as much power as necessary. They were well aware of space and energy, knew where their bodies began and ended, as well as those of their opponents in *kumite*, or sparring practice. In contrast, beginner white and yellow belts keen to prove their fledgling fighting prowess—often with an agenda of suppressed anger, resentment or macho pride—were dangerous loose cannons, who often unintentionally hurt themselves and others. It's the reason some martial arts clubs require beginners to spend countless hours on punching bags, padded dummies and buckets of sand before allowing them to take part in open *kumite* training sessions.

Likewise, when anger in an individual is acknowledged and has been discharged, that person is far safer than someone who is afraid to explore and discharge his anger, or who denies that he has powerful suppressed feelings of aggression. Outside of therapy, sport is a perfect, relatively safe outlet for aggression.

How can I stop playing?

It's not by trying to kill our Characters that we stop them running or inter-fering in our lives. Hating or resisting them will only make them stronger. Characters at one time helped us survive, so it is healthier to acknowledge their help and *then* to transcend them. It is even possible to enlist their help in present time.

The way through is by teasing apart the Character and discharging its unresolved emotion. Source it—where and when did it first arise? What part of our nature, what instinct—such as fight or flight or freeze—did it follow? Experience its energy without resistance, without pushing away the uncomfortable emotions, so there is nothing to which it can stick. Observe its dynamics, how it operates. Get to know its script and its agenda. What was its purpose? Objectify it so you can see it as a part of you, but not the whole you. Then, when you *know* it is not you—when you know it is not how you would consciously run things—take over and do it your way.

As we will see in a later chapter, the Drama Triangle can be played at a much higher and more positive level when people step out of their Charac-ters and into their Higher Selves.

11

Addicted to our Characters

There is often unconscious resistance, even emotional pain, when we decide we want to drop Characters and empower ourselves once more—especially from the Victim Character. Based on the experience of being victimised, the script the Character is following says that empowerment means *abuse of power*. Our true Self, however, just wants to be an effective human being.

However, before we become aware enough of our Characters to want to drop them, we may identify so strongly with one Character that we consciously suppress any deviation from the rigid dictates of who we think we are. This Character 'works' for us. It gives us the power or the control over people and situations that we feel we need in a world perceived as hostile. Alternatively, if it is a disempowered Character, such as Poor Me or Battler, it simply enables an unchallenging life of familiarity and stability, and the control factor comes from covert or unconscious manipulation of others' emotions. The emergence of a different Character is seen as a threat to the stability and predictability of our world. We may then find we have a Stuck Character, where our conscious will becomes involved in *not* changing.

Toxic Characters

The person who appears to be stuck in one Character all her life and who rarely, if ever, flips generally has an enormous amount of suppressed energy below the surface, held there with rigid force. Stuck Characters tend to be toxic because they are so deceptive to themselves as well as others. Let's say the person has a Nice Character. You know the one—she never raises her voice and is always sweetly offering to help everyone. Naturally people exploit her and take advantage of her good will, but she refuses to change. Or he's the office Good Guy always willing to cover for others' slips and omissions. In spite of this, somehow things always seem to go wrong with this Character. His help is not sought because people always feel worse afterwards, and his cover-ups are somehow leaked to the boss and his mates get into trouble while he stands by blameless.

A variation on this is the Character who Can't Say No, who takes on far more than he can effectively achieve just to get approval. When he fails to deliver on his promises, others end up having to cover for him. Beneath his inability to set boundaries for himself, this Character wants to be the Go-To Guy. He *wants* to be able to deliver, and will push himself past his ability to cope with the volume of things people give him to do. At the same time, he resents that people take advantage of his compliant nature. Resentment and anger are something he can't admit—he's a Nice Guy, so he denies and suppresses his prickly emotions. The anger creates a Vicious flipside which only shows in the actual results of his actions. He himself is totally unaware that his hidden resentment is exposed in the chaos and confusion of his failed promises. Outwardly he appears to be a Stuck Character who never flips. And everyone agrees that he is so 'nice' that he'd never intentionally hurt a fly.

Is it her or is it me?

When we feel the energy coming from a Nice Character we often experience a confusing double message. Her attitude is sweet and compliant and helpful, but our gut reaction can be uneasy. With a little experience we can actually feel the suppressed resentment in her belly, detect the saccharine quality of her smile. Trust your gut reaction. The Nice Character is in denial, suppressing unacceptable emotions such as her own angry resentment. Then she will unconsciously project it onto those around her. She'll be blameless, but you may end up as collateral damage.

It takes a lot of provocation to flip a Nice Character. She will probably be upset first and angry as her very last resort. Only if she realises her cover is blown and too many people see her as covertly nasty—something she believes deep down and fears—will she begin to consider changing, and then only if she feels supported. The defences are strong. Even in therapy, in a setting of compassion and acceptance, it takes a lot of work to gradually draw out her suppressed anger and facilitate its discharge.

Oops, it *is* me!

Then, of course, we might discover that *we* are being the Nice Character, instead of the nice person we think we are. There is suppressed anger we don't want to own or ever experience, and it's a painful self-reckoning until we can allow its safe and healthy expression. A prodigious amount of car-screaming, pillow-bashing or bag-punching—preferably on our own so we don't have to worry about others' reactions—can do wonders. Try it sometime! At first, the very thought of doing this is scary. We fear losing control, going berserk, and being taken away by men in white coats. Physical exercise is a good way to start, because it brings our physical energy up enough to handle strong emotion, and gives us the means to express it.

We do need to feel we are safe and that others are safe with us. Anger is so much more explosive when it has been concentrated by suppression. When anger is expressed without resistance it is a clean emotion and powerful to feel as it leaves us—as long as no-one, and no property, gets damaged. If we do damage property, we're still in Destructive Character mode. When we suppress anger we can become depressed, especially if we feel we have to pretend to be Nice.

It really is okay to be human. Our natural emotions have a place too.

I need it, why can't I let myself have it?

The Must Have/Can't Have Character 'must have' something—say, a solution to her problems. She appears actively to seek it and might ask anyone she meets for solutions. Or her asking for help will seem implicit in her constant complaining. However, when offered a range of feasible solutions, she 'can't have' any of them. She can't make them work or see them as relevant or her style. Nor has she been able to find any solutions herself—the problem is too huge and would take far more energy than she's got to do anything about it, which is also why she can't accept solutions from anyone else. Because it has defeated her, she feels no-one else understands the complexity of the whole problem, either.

Using the block 'Yes, but', she would rather *have* her problem than change anything. Her inability to take responsibility for her situation condemns her to becoming her own worst problem. She probably gets quite a lot of attention by this unconscious mechanism, especially from Compulsive Helpers who are drawn like magnets to hopeless causes.

The Fizzler

The Must Have/Can't Have Character has several variations, including the Fizzler Character exemplified in 38-year-old Dimitri, whose law career had shown early promise, then fizzled. As a child Dimitri was frequently compared to his talented younger brother Alex, to whom achievements came easily. Dimitri had always believed Alex was favoured over him, while his brother's slip-ups were usually considered Dimitri's fault.

Despite coming to the conclusion that nothing he could do would win favour, a Character emerged that took on every possible project and gave 150 per cent effort in everything he did, hoping for brownie points. It had worked early in his career and he had built an impressive reputation as a go-getter and high-achiever.

However, it all came crashing down when he became infected with a mysterious virus after an overseas holiday and was ill for weeks. Returning to work, he doubled his efforts to catch up and added to the number of cases he was used to handling, only to collapse within a fortnight. Months of bed-rest followed during which he was unable to work, sometimes unable even to get up. A raft of medical tests revealed nothing conclusive, but the unspecified diagnoses of 'auto-immune disorder', 'blood parasites' and chronic fatigue were to dog him for over a decade. Nutritional supplements helped, but as soon as he felt strong enough to work he overdid the effort and came crashing down once more. It was the Fizzler Character.

The Fizzler is a syndrome of conditioned, high-effort behaviours which worked briefly but have failed for far longer. In experiments on how positive and negative reinforcement affect learning, rats will increase behaviour that once got them a reward. Even when the reward of a pellet of food is substituted by the punishment of an electric shock, the rat will increase the formerly effective behaviour until, eventually, that behaviour ceases.

Dimitri's efforts to 'get brownie points' were similar to the rat in the experiment. Even when there was no possible reward for the work he was doing—it was neither paid nor acknowledged, nor, in some cases, even known that his work had formed the basis of a successful project—Dimitri was compelled to put in effort which actually made him ill with exhaustion. Part of this Character syndrome was that he was unable to receive compliments when they were freely given. He would at times exaggerate to others his contribution to a project, but strangely, when he *was* acknowledged, he minimised his own input while maximising that of others. It was an echo of how his parents treated him and his little brother when they were children.

In the same vein, Dimitri chose partners in both romance and business ventures who were unable to appreciate his deeper values and qualities, or the extra effort he put into relationships. Moulding himself to his partner's preferences, he denied his own and the relationships soon failed. In everything, Dimitri found it supremely difficult to ask for or accept help. The worst phases of his illness were downward spirals of helplessness. Only after intensive therapeutic work on self-esteem and practice in doing what was good for him did this vicious cycle begin slowly to change.

The most significant improvements occurred with a change in his career. Being a lawyer was his parents' choice, while his new field combines many of the things he loves and has never allowed himself. Even so, he still has to monitor his automatic tendency to take on too much.

The Fizzler Character has no brakes. After early promise, the only thing that will stop his increasingly ineffective effort is when he crashes and burns. Dimitri has to remember to pace himself, to acknowledge himself and simply to enjoy what he is doing in the present.

Nothing works for me!

A variation on Must Have/Can't Have is Nothing Works for Me. This is a toxic Character who seeks help for a problem, be it in their health, finances or a possession that needs fixing, but the solution never works to fix the problem. Frequently they doubt any remedy even as they are given it, with what looks like (and is) an obstinate refusal to be helped. Helpers soon notice that the Nothing Works for Me Character either ignores instructions or follows them incorrectly, causing further complications. Then they'll seek solutions to that complication, getting further and further away from the real source of the problem.

The Nothing Works for Me Character often has a very skewed, cynical view of the world. They typically believe the worst and doubt anyone has a benign motive for what they do. They might believe in conspiracies, or that businesses exist for the sole purpose of fleecing unwary consumers.

Erica, aged 68, had an extreme Nothing Works for Me Character. She lived on her own, battling with many unfixed things in her home and her life. One day she fell and broke her hip. Because she erroneously believed that having more than one phone extension would cost her extra, she only had one handset, and this was at the other end of the house to where she had fallen. Erica's hip was broken so badly, she could not move. It was two days before she was able to alert the attention of a passer-by, after which she was taken to hospital. Her son Bernard, who lived in another city, had left messages on her phone, but was used to his mother not returning his calls. She would say she wanted to save on the expense of making phone calls. A week later the social worker at the hospital rang Bernard to ask about discharge details. It was the first time he knew Erica was injured and in hospital. On admission, Erica had given no details of next of kin, while complaining to her ward-mates that her family had forgotten her.

Erica refused Bernard's offer for her to convalesce with him and his wife, as well as the offer of a home nurse to visit her in her own house, saying that neither would work out. The hospital sent her to a nursing home to recover, where she complained that her son had just wanted to dump her and forget her.

By the time her hip had healed enough for her to return home in a wheel-chair, Bernard had installed three extension phone lines for her, as well as a cordless phone she could carry with her at all times. Erica pulled out all the extensions, complaining that they used extra electricity and cost extra 'line rental'. One day when Bernard rang her, she took a long time to get to the phone. He asked her why she did not have her cordless. Erica said it didn't work. Her son arranged for the phone to be fixed, but the repairman could find nothing wrong with it. Eventually, Bernard worked out that Erica had never re-charged it. Erica believed that if it cost money to charge, it wasn't worth it. Despite this, concerned for his mother's safety, Bernard bought her a mobile phone, made sure she charged it and knew how it worked. Erica dropped some food on it one day and put it in the washing machine to clean it. The phone came apart in the wash and a piece of plastic got stuck in the rotor of the machine. This was only discovered by the repairman Bernard sent, when she complained that her washing machine had broken down. Bernard ended up paying for a new washing machine. He gave up on the mobile phone, and told his mother that he would pay for the 'extra lines' as long as she allowed him to plug the land line extensions back in again. Even so, he often finds she has unplugged them 'to save money'.

This is only one episode in Bernard's ongoing struggle to get badly needed help to his mother. Erica does not have dementia. She simply has a chronic Nothing Works for Me Character. It has operated all her life, and the longer she acts it out, the more it is reinforced. It has got a great deal worse as she's aged and is not as able to look after herself. Her original unsolved problems have compounded into multiple layers of complications, like the incorrectly and partially healed calcifications in her broken hip that could have been avoided had she been taken to hospital immediately. The break took far longer to heal than normal, has slowed down her walking and aches with arthritis. She now rarely attempts getting out of her wheelchair.

The space around Erica is fractious with her resistance to life, making people feel irritable in her presence. Feeling this one day when replacing her fused toaster for the sixth time, Bernard exclaimed in frustration that electrical appliances just broke down as soon as they saw her coming. Erica's beliefs about people's self-serving motives end up coming true when helpers give up in defeat.

Erica's Nothing Works for Me Character was born when she was a child and believed she was responsible for the unspoken fury and friction between her parents. She concluded she must be the worst person in the world, worthless and useless. Because she had failed to help her parents, she reasoned, no-one would ever be able to help her. By the time she was 60, she had long made this a self-fulfilling prophecy, alienating most people who tried to get close and cynically convinced the world was a crock.

The Nothing Works for Me Character is one of the most toxic and can have a disastrous effect on helpers, as they are determined to make everyone who tries to help them fail too. Recognising this may save helpers from being sucked into this Character's toxic spiral.

I'm so keen when I start, but then I lose interest!

We might have a Character with a purpose that has apparent enthusiasm in beginning a project, but is short-lived. The Fast-Fader Character becomes discouraged as soon as we meet the slightest obstacle—whereupon we give up with a dejected 'What's the use?' Then we hate ourselves, first for having no stamina and secondly for having tried in the first place. Usually we hate feeling this way and so begin to deny that the project ever mattered to us. At that point we have flipped into an Apathetic Character.

Apathy is a state of simply not caring, and is the deadliest of all energies because it gravitates to lower and lower levels and 'sucks' the energy from those around as well. If an enthusiastic friend can inspire our Apathetic Character to start something new once more, our inspiration soon fails and we flip back into Apathy because we are not self-determined. We cannot successfully be motivated unless it's from the Higher Self. Outside influences will rarely work for long. The Fast-Fader and its Apathetic flipside are closely related to the Must Have/Can't Have syndrome. To get ourselves out of an Apathetic Character we need to do the very thing the Character does not want to do—get moving and do some exercise. Exercise literally breaks rigidified astral structures. Get the endorphins flowing in the brain, and we will feel better. Our energy and purpose will return.

The Chaos Merchant

Rod was a powerbroker CEO with a Chaos Merchant Character who specialised in sending Covertly Hostile flunkies into rival companies to white-ant them with gossip, miscommunication and incompetence, upon which he would take the then-failing companies over. He ruled his own companies with an unpredictable Tyrant Character, keeping his staff 'on their toes', so he said, by alternately coldly undercutting them and treating them with extraordinary generosity and personal attention. They never knew where they stood, and feared him as much as they admired him.

The Vampire Character

Another toxic Character which likes to operate behind the scenes is the Energetic Vampire, as in the case of Max. A lead salesman with consistently high monthly statistics, everyone believed him to be the calmest member of the sales team. When others were frantic with stress due to approaching deadlines and unfilled quotas, Max was serene and relaxed. When other sales-people became furious or disappointed with clients who did not re-order,

Max would offer to talk them into re-ordering and they often did. Some time later, these clients would transfer to Max's list. Max never got angry. Skilfully and unobtrusively he would foment anger in his sales team. When they exploded with frustration, Max would energetically feed on this volatile energy while remaining calm. Much like a sociopath, he would manipulate others to give him the energy (and entertainment) he needed, while everyone believed the angry ones were at fault and he was beyond reproach. Max justified his actions with the firm conviction that he was superior to everyone else, and enjoyed his power-ploys immensely, if privately. While he believed he was in control of the Character, he was unable to gain enough detachment from it ever to see how it drove him.

Are we 'addicted' to our Characters?

In most cases, yes. We can be addicted to patterns of behaviour as much as to toxic substances. Characters share similar energetic structures in our subtle bodies to other kinds of addictions, with the same result: amplifying or deadening emotions and eroding our will.

There are differences, too, of course. Drugs of addiction are initially pleasurable, but as tolerance increases, the addict needs more and more *just to feel normal.* A Character develops to help us survive difficult situations. In time, only the Character's behaviour feels normal, though it is very far from the real us.

The initial function of an addictive substance is to give pleasure and displace pain, anxiety or boredom. However, because it simply displaces discomfort and does not actually address the underlying need, it creates a false structure built on an illusion. It has its own dynamic of a closed-loop system, feeding its own escapist motivation like a snake biting its own tail and resisting conscious attempts to change it.

Addictions add to the layers of unconsciousness around *samskaras.* To the person experiencing this trance-like state, it feels like it reduces stress in the entire nervous system, similar to anaesthetic during a surgical or dental procedure. However, our Characters and addictions simply divert our attention from our underlying problems and thus prevent their resolution. Each creates oblivious, automatic behaviour which ends up being more harmful than effective. The more dominant our Characters and addictions, the less our real Self can have a life. We think we are making our own choices, when nothing could be further from the truth.

The Shut-In Character

Shut-in kids are currently a widespread problem in Japan causing alarm among parents, social workers and schools. Mainly teenagers, they simply stay in their rooms, sometimes for years. For the determined Shut-In, no inducement, threat or rational argument will tempt him out of his self-imposed isolation. It frequently leads to suicide.

The Shut-In Character resembles the fairy story of the Sleeping Beauty, or the Princess in the Tower. The fable's guardian dragon, ogre or witch represents parental control, expectations and demands. The castle tower itself is the isolation of the youngster's room. The surrounding barrier of thickets of thorns equates to his limitations and social phobia. The rescuer Prince translates as any means by which the Shut-In enables him- or herself eventually to escape self-imposed incarceration.

The fairy story is an appropriate analogy, because identification with Fantasy or Fairytale Characters is so much a part of these kids' lives. Many Shut-Ins find an outlet in the Internet, and conversely, they have often become Shut-Ins due to an addiction to online gaming, particularly role-play games. A Mecca for Characters, the Internet makes it even more difficult to adjust to real life and find a real identity due to an imbalance of addictive astral features divorced from the physical and etheric bodies.

What shut-in kids learn about their world and their environment has a unique slant. Through the Internet, the information available for their education is theoretically limitless, interest-driven and without any formal structure, but all the information that they access is filtered through their social phobia. Education for a shut-in means that they remain passive, the most active part of their life being their imagination. There are few reality checks, and Characters abound in the avatars kids choose to mask their identities in chatrooms and forums.

Internet Junkies

The world of the Internet is unique. It is still predominantly a world of the young, those who cut their teeth on keyboards, learned to type before they learned to print by hand and rely on spell-check rather than looking up a dictionary. It's a different mindset to those of the pre-digital age, perhaps even a mind on another level of evolution. It's the kind of thinking that often has more of an affinity for technology than for human values, and thrives in virtual environments where instant gratification is *apparently* more frequently possible than not.

Todd was a prodigy at chess, music and computers, became a bullied Geek at school, then became a Shut-In who hacked into his school database to falsify attendance records. Designing websites soon became a paying concern, but he made more money playing online poker and gave up designing to adopt a Web Entrepreneur Role. At 21, he bought his first condominium and brokered a domain sale, both for six figures. Shortly after this, big losses at poker steered him to his other addiction—online role-play games, which he currently plays for six to eight hours a day. He works for three hours a day, and boasts that he earns more in a month than his college professor father earns in a year.

Todd sees no reason to go to university, to work hard, to read books or to value friendships. His Web Entrepreneur Role has survived well so far in an opportunistic world of people who rarely keep agreements and who enjoy making fools of people with an old-fashioned work ethic. He believes he is creating effective Roles in his life, but in truth they are one Escapist Character after another. The only thing to tell him he's not living the dream he has fantasised is his online blog and the self-reflection it offers, of lethargy, boredom and lack of motivation.

There is a natural separation—an even bigger communication gap than in pre-Internet generations—between congenitally computer-literate youth and the relatively technologically challenged adults of their parents' generation. This includes a gap in all the normal interactive social skills with which the older generation grew up, and which many young people neatly avoid in electronic cyber-universes, in forums where the median age of its denizens is fourteen to sixteen. These are kids who don't go outside to meet friends. They meet in social networking sites, chatrooms, forums and blogs, present themselves publicly through Facebook or MySpace, and use Instant Messaging and email. They develop relationships which might last for years but are more often brief, without having met in the flesh, or ever wanting to meet.

They get to know each other by invitation to read each other's blogs. It's a strange intimacy because there's no etheric component. Without the non-verbal, unwritten information that comes from sensing energy or reading body language and facial expressions, a great deal of human interaction is sliced off. But it's as immediate and compelling as reality TV, even more so with the addition of webcams to Instant Messaging conversations. An apparent lack of visible consequences also entails little responsibility.

If not complete shut-ins, there's a growing tendency among young people all over the developed world to withdraw from the real world into seclusion, especially where the Internet offers a virtual universe of both more distraction and fewer real-life challenges. In Japan, they are called *otaku*, meaning those who stay at home and have no life apart from online gaming. It's a pejorative term, usually followed by 'sad loser'. Typically they avoid communication with the outside world, except online, and prefer to use abbreviated textese without punctuation. It appears to reflect life in the technological age, where we receive so much information in such concentrated bursts that our expression must truncate itself. We shut out whatever we feel is extraneous, but also what is too much to absorb. It's a situation that creates Fantasy Characters within Characters such as Geeks and Gamers.

Escaping from problematic family and other relationships into a world of fantasy games, with the pseudo challenges of those virtual worlds, addictions to online role-play games such as World of Warcraft are common, where real-life achievements are substituted with fantasy status, gold and equipment. Such games hold huge attractions for teenagers with social phobias and disempowered Characters. It's not unusual for those who have normal, healthy lives when they first start World of Warcraft to lose jobs and girlfriends, and fail at school or university. It is seen as *the* most addictive game in history and has led to deaths from starvation and lack of sleep.

Quite apart from online role-play games, the overwhelming pull of the Internet has much to do with an imbalance of astral and etheric components. In fact the Internet could be seen as the province of astrality without boundaries, so divorced from the etheric and physical for them to be irrelevant. In its virtual components our experience of the Internet mimics a spiritual universe, where travel and connection with others is at the speed of thought, but one that is sadly lacking in Egoic or actual spiritual presence. Instant information, instant virtual travel, instant communication with those across the globe (or at the next desk) means those elements which anchor us in human experience and in present time—namely, our physical bodies, our energy and our physical environment—are absent. Without a grounding in the physical and the etheric, being in present time is almost impossible. There is a danger that the concentration of astral elements—thoughts, the imagination, emotions without an etheric platform, fantasy and addictive pseudo-worlds filled with like-minded Internet Junkie Characters—could ultimately divorce users from their spiritual potential and even from their humanity, as effectively as crack cocaine. There is no socially diverse community to balance such experiences, to give meaning to effort and achievement, to overcome one's own lethargy or lack of motivation. It's the path of least resistance—and this has never enabled impressive evolution.

By no means are all users of the Internet so affected, of course, but the young are especially vulnerable to its attractions. It's not a reason to dismiss the many benefits of the Internet, but it is a rapidly growing area in which to be aware of Character traps.

The only way I can be real . . .

On the other hand, because of the missing etheric element, the Internet is the main platform of communication with the outside world for people with autism. It is human interaction without any blood or breath in it, and optional sound. The impact of what is coming in can be modulated, buffered or deleted at the touch of a key. For people in the autism spectrum, who find human facial expressions baffling or incomprehensible, whose brains can be wired in extreme or selective left-brain logic coupled with huge fear of the unfamiliar and a very low threshold tolerance of noise, the written communication of the Internet is a godsend. It allows them an arena through forums, IM and email to develop their prodigious intelligence and explore areas of interest without fear of judgment or non-acceptance, with each other and with non-autists as well. It's their bridge to the normal world, one in which they can control the degree of information (noise) coming in at no risk of being overwhelmed, and often the only place in which they can feel real.

Whose addiction is it?

I smoked cigarettes for twenty years before I gave them up. Seven years after I had my last cigarette, I was meditating when I experienced a sudden, intense desire for a cigarette. I knew *I* didn't want a cigarette or to smoke, having overcome both the physical and the psychological aspects of my addiction years before. I went back into meditation to source the compelling thought and realised I was catching the thoughts and desires of the man in the house next door. I learned later this man was dying of emphysema after a lifetime of smoking. When I had momentarily lost focus in my meditation, I also lost the structure which allowed my Higher Self predominance over the imprinted desires of my astral body. There was evidently enough of the 'smoker' imprint in my astral body to resonate with my neighbour's addiction—even after seven years. It was a sobering thought.

We all have our own cravings and addictions. They can be contagious, especially if we have already imprinted that addiction on our astral body. Having created an addictive astral structure which automatically takes us on the same behavioural path, even years after the physical addiction has stopped, a similar energy in our environment can set it off.

It's exactly the same with our Characters. We can fall into old habits if we're not fully aware and don't consciously take them over. It's why drug rehab programs encourage recovering addicts to change their habitual lifestyle—to keep away from old friends who are still living the old addicted lifestyle and change their environment to one that is conducive to new, positive choices. Once our *samskaras* have been discharged, freeing us from layers of conditioning, it is easier to create new, healthier patterns of behaviour. We find there's less need to compensate, anaesthetise or self-medicate through addictive substances or mesmeric behaviours, but conscious effort and intention are still required.

The astral body is full of habits good and bad. It can pull us in all directions like a whirlpool. But when we choose to be more conscious of the choices we are making, we can decide not to get pulled under.

Our astral body's ability to take imprints and reinforce them can be utilised for healthy choices if we can find a positive habit to substitute for the old addiction. For example, it's difficult to start jogging if we've never done it. But if we make that decision and stick to it as a regular daily routine, it's far easier to roll out of bed into running shoes and hit the track than if we decide just to do it whenever we feel like it. Similarly with our Characters. Once we cultivate the habit of not reacting, it's far easier to stay out of them.

Getting out of the whirlpool

Though the habitual emotional pulls of our astral body can distract us from living our own lives, there is still our Egoic body, the vehicle of the Higher Self which links us with the real us. Our Egoic body is the closest to who we are as eternal beings and furthest from our physical bodies. It is the body that is closest to Spirit. In it we may experience *Being*, a state of knowing we are one with all creation through all time.

When in the Ego we do not think—we *know*. It is a knowingness that is beyond thought or memory because it is not limited by our brain or mind. Instead of the astral body's reactive emotions, conditioned by our past, we can have the Ego's unconditional feelings, profound, present and yet timeless. These feelings are so different to our normal grasping way of interacting with our environment that they require some getting used to.

We are so accustomed to the grasping feeling of reactive emotions in our Character universe that we can become addicted to running on the nervous energy this produces. It's only when we've become used to being *non-reactive* that we feel how disruptive and illusory reactive emotions are. This is not to say reactive emotions are not real—they are intense and real— but their causes might be something that happened when we were perhaps three years old. They have continued to happen, at intervals, since then, triggered by associations in the environment or attracted by the resonating vibrations of our *samskaras*, and have been added to by many other past experiences. Reacting in adulthood as a three-year-old might is the part that is inappropriate—and ineffective as well.

The power of being on the brink

For those who have developed an awareness by self-observation, there is a short moment of time when we realise with clarity that we are having an emotional reaction, and in which we also see what we would usually do, and what will happen if we default into a Character's habitual behaviour. On this brink, we can make a decision to indulge in acting out a reactive emotion, or not.

A Character's behaviour is always predictable, so if we can take a moment and step back, pre-play that behaviour out in our minds and see what the inevitable outcome will be, it's often enough to allow us the choice of *not* indulging in the reaction. The difference in outcome to what usually happens is frequently astounding and illuminating.

However, there are times when we are more 'in' Characters than others. Possibly it's fatigue or stress, or the Character has been strongly triggered by an external event. The best we can do in such circumstances is learn more about the reactive pattern in retrospect, try not to fall into shame, blame, regret and failure as we watch it all happen as scripted, and work out a better stratagem for the next time we might be triggered.

Once we have sourced a Character and identified its attributes and thought patterns, if we are entering a situation which would normally trigger that Character, it's possible to prepare a conscious Role instead, in which we can be more present and in control. We can pause, as it were, in the wings before going on stage, determining that we will not be a Character—and choose instead the scary option of being spontaneous and unscripted: to improvise within a certain preferred, non-reactive platform.

The joy of spontaneity

Initially it can be frightening, but spontaneity is fun. It's a great deal more fun than a scripted play which unfolds every night in the same way, with the same result and the same ending, and far more enjoyable than the dysfunction of a Character-scripted life. Spontaneity that is truly non-reactive and from the Ego is likely to be, instead, appropriate action and response.

The rigidity of a Character's energy feels like a safe scaffolding we are unwilling to let go of, for fear of what might happen. Like a substance addiction it is a crutch which holds us back rather than holding us up.

When we begin to interact with people non-reactively, it feels strange. Without the familiar astral pulls and pushes, we might feel a little at sea. The strangeness might be enough to send us back into reactive mode, back into a Character which prefers not to take responsibility.

Put attention instead on how calm and in control you feel, despite a certain unfamiliarity. Enjoy the clarity of mind. Stay in present time by using the physical universe (touching solid objects, feeling their mass, texture, temperature) to ground you, to connect you to present time. Being in the present allows more awareness. When our attention is no longer trapped in holding the past at bay, more of our attention is available for us to use. We can be effective without hiding behind a Character.

Like learning to ride a surfboard, we might wobble and fall before becoming stable. In a Role we can often see what's coming and take effective action. In a Role we are not as affected by other people's emotions. Not that we won't feel what others feel—often we can feel it more profoundly than when in the tunnel-visioned narcissism of a Character. We feel it empathically and are able to leave it with them, rather than sympathetically, when we mistakenly identify with a Character's emotion, or make judgments about people for what they are going through. Without Characters we can feel for someone without taking their baggage on board. We can remain supportive while allowing others to have their own journey. After all, if we were to take on someone else's process, we help neither them nor ourselves.

Without Characters we are free to be whomever we want to be. We can discover who we really are.

PART II

Onwards and upwards:
Roles

The Guest

The Guest is inside you, and also inside me;
You know the sprout is hidden inside the seed.
We are all struggling; none of us has gone far.
Let your arrogance go, and look around inside.

The blue sky opens out farther and farther.
The daily sense of failure goes away,
The damage I have done to myself fades,
A million suns come forward with light,
When I sit firmly in that world.

Kabir (1440–1518)

12

The spiritual path

Since the musical Hair burst onto the stage in 1967, much of the world
has become aware of New Age spirituality and its search for spiritual truth
and enlightenment outside of traditional, organised religions. From theoso-
phists to hippies, to psychic fairs where you may have your aura read and
photographed, your fortune told and your spirit guides drawn for you in
pastel crayons, New Agers bring a host of Spiritual Characters. Many believe
that in this arena we can trust people to have more integrity and benevolence towards others than in other areas.

Wherever there are Characters, however, there is self-deception. Others
also will inevitably be deceived. Perhaps more than any other area of life,
we need discernment and to take responsibility for not letting ourselves be
fooled.

Among the few genuine gurus and many true seekers, sincerity alone
in the seeker or the teacher is no guarantee that truth is being offered, any
more than in older scripture-based religions who swear theirs is the one
true faith. The Spiritual Character may have the appearance of a devotee of
any form of spiritual practice, old or new. The robes, veils and mitres, the
incense, crystals and beads are often the image and paraphernalia of sacred
practice rather than spirituality of any depth. Similarly, the attitude and
lifestyle of a Spiritual Character has certain aspects that might be expected:
they may practise meditation, yoga postures, tai chi or qi gong; they may be
vegetarian, mild of manner and good-hearted. They may believe in reincar-
nation, astrology, tarot and other oracles.

True spirituality is not about appearances. They are as superficial and deceptive as the robes of a paedophile priest.

'It must have been meant to happen'

A popular belief among Spiritual Characters is that if something is meant to happen, it will, easily and without effort. It's a bit like magical thinking, based on a conviction that angelic beings are orchestrating our lives through apparent coincidence and synchronicity. It's a convenient delusion that allows us to be fatalistic, a pseudo-acceptance of our fate where we do not take responsibility for changing what needs to be changed.

Paradoxically, when I ask these same Eternal Seekers about periods in their lives when they have grown the most, they will invariably reply that it was when they struggled against obstacles, and that striving against difficulty has made them strong, compassionate and wise. Often the two conflicting ideas co-exist in these Characters side by side. One, however, is based on belief without much evidence, while the other is based in experience.

Without denying that good fortune sometimes lands unexpectedly, the life path of incarnated beings is one of mastering the gravity, mass, pressure and linear time of the physical universe. We would never have learned to walk otherwise. It means we learn about the need for planning, organising, persistence and effort and a myriad other physical universe realities *before* we learn about allowing and letting go what needs to be let go, that we are actually made of light, that we create our reality, and that time is not linear. Once we have overcome, we can become. It's the unique lesson of incarnation.

We could look at this material universe as one where our lessons include mastering our thoughts and emotions so they are not merely reactive or instinctual. If we are tuning our aspirations to a higher octave and aiming for the most evolved we can possibly be, our conscious intention could take us to quite a different destiny—one we create ourselves, in line with the best of our human potential. That truly is the 'way we were meant to be'.

The Spiritual Healer Character

Among Spiritual Characters, many a Victim Character evolves into a Compulsive Helper masquerading as a Healer. From there, if they are charismatic and successful, they may aim for Guru or Spiritual Teacher. If we are still in Character mode, it is almost impossible to discern whether a spiritual teacher is a true Healer, a Guru, a Scamster or just a Character in delusion. If we are in a Needy Character or a naive, trusting Follower or Devotee Character, we will not see how our guru deceives himself and others.

There are plenty of Spiritual Characters—Healers, Teachers, Motivational and Inspirational Speakers of traditions new and old—who charge exorbitantly with no good evidence of value except in the hopes of desperate seekers. There's not a great deal of difference between these and some high-profile investment and stock-market gurus or holders of 'life-changing' financial seminars, all of whom manifest their wealth through an effortless transfer from your wallet to their gold-plated money-clip. Be judicious before you spend your well-earned coin on someone who seems to have something you think you lack!

Eternal Seeker, Workshop Junkie

Peter went to every New Age group he could find. He sometimes saw three different kinds of spiritual or holistic practitioners weekly. Naturally he found they frequently conflicted, and he blamed them for his inability to make any of their techniques work, rather than taking responsibility for his own disempowered Dependent Character. On occasion Peter stormed out of the practitioner's room without paying, shouting insults about their 'bullshit'. Peter's Nothing Works for Me Character was determined to show that no-one could help him, demanding others take over for him and rejecting them almost in the same breath. The crux of Peter's desperation was his unconscious self-hatred, projected onto those around him.

John also religiously attended meditation groups and healing workshops, after which he would effusively gush about how amazing the energy was and how many energy 'blocks' he had shifted. His life was going to be so different now. The trouble was, John never practised meditation on his own. The gains he made faded because he didn't take responsibility for his own evolution, relying instead on the next guru and the next group.

The Guru and the Devotee

Pitted against Group and Workshop Junkies is frequently the Guru Character, who can never admit to not knowing an answer or to being wrong, while her students must accept her gently spoken suggestions as God-given truth. She manipulates them emotionally with confrontational information from a pseudo-spiritual reality. She simply says she's 'on a higher level' and that they 'cannot see the Truth'. It puts her followers into confusion, not allowing them to trust their own judgment.

The Guru cannot exist without followers. Her apparent certainty and serenity attract the uncertain and disempowered as Devotees, who want to be like her. Wanting what she has, they believe that if they do what she says they will achieve self-mastery. Ironically, in projecting guru-hood onto a spiritual leader instead of owning their own wisdom, followers can experience her teachings as benevolent and illuminating, and her presence as healing. They are literally creating her higher status in order to help themselves evolve spiritually, because they do not feel confident enough to do so themselves—yet.

Eleanor has a Guru Character that is powerful and creative. Naive, good-hearted and sincere Devotee Characters defer to Eleanor's opinion on everything from whether they should marry so-and-so to what colour car to buy. Clearly, they have given her their power, and it will be a long road, riddled with disillusionment, before they can wrench it back again.

In the traditions of ancient Eastern religions, none could be enlightened by their own efforts. It took the guru's *shaktipat*—the transfer of grace from an Enlightened One. Many believe this no longer applies and that in the twenty-first century we are responsible for our own enlightenment.

Each of us has an Inner Self Helper. Contacting this part of ourselves enables us to be our own guru and take responsibility for our lives ourselves. To do this, devotees need to validate their own perceptions and decisions *as they are learning,* and reverse the idea that a guru alone has access to Higher Truth—without rejecting her or her teachings automatically.

Taking responsibility for ourselves means, too, that we no longer expect others to change. Paradoxically, however, in changing ourselves and our attitudes, we can miraculously change the way others relate to us. It is difficult, ongoing work, but by empowering ourselves in this way we free not only ourselves from the Character trap, but the Guru and anyone else with power over us.

Discerning Truth
(when we're not enlightened yet)

It's true that in order to evolve personally and spiritually, the conditioned personality needs to be deconstructed and then reconstructed with more truth. It's also true that often we cannot see what specifically is not authentic in ourselves, and we will habitually ask for that information from someone to whom we have attributed more enlightenment. We can frequently be deluded about a teacher's true worth—often we expect too much in our projection of perfection onto our teachers. We thus doom ourselves to disappointment as well as disillusionment, sometimes and mistakenly, about spirituality itself.

The more we are in our true Selves the more we can discern Truth in others around us. Through trial and error, through commitment to a path that seems true to us, we begin gradually to know for ourselves.

The real Truth is that everyone has to decide their own true path for themselves, which does not exclude using wise and brilliant teachers as a resource. A true Teacher will enable students to discover their own inner wisdom and not demand that they necessarily follow the same path.

Responsibility and blame

Solange came in, furious from seeing her alternative health practitioner. Her chronic health problems had been improving, but now the remedies seemed no longer to be effective. The practitioner had become annoyed with her, telling her she was sabotaging herself and that she was responsible for her situation. Not only had she caused all her own health issues, he said, but she had attracted all the tragedy in her life which had made her susceptible to poor health. Solange felt she had suffered a great deal in her life through situations and events that were not of her causing, and now, not only was the practitioner refusing to help her, but his Rescuer had gone into Persecutor, blaming her for things she was not able to control.

Solange said what had infuriated her most was his saying she was responsible for making herself sick. She hotly compared him to the sort of person who thought all those who died on 9/11 brought it on themselves.

115

She felt it was far too simplistic to say that people brought disasters and abuse on themselves, or that God was punishing them or that they deserved to be punished.

I agreed that people certainly don't *intend* to make themselves ill, or to have bad luck. Unconsciously, however, we can draw bad luck towards us by habitual negative thinking. Solange was obviously angry not only at the practitioner, but also life's unfairness. She was confusing blame and responsibility. It took a short illustration to show her what I meant.

If your locked car were stolen, it wouldn't be your fault. It's in the category of *shit happens*. Once gone, it wouldn't do you any good to jump up and down screaming for the thief to return it. Nor would it help to keep on crying forever about the loss.

However, though it's not your fault, it is your *responsibility* to deal with it, because the car is your property. In taking responsibility you notify your insurance company and the police. You learn some new skills, including dealing with bureaucratic rigmaroles, and you have to take responsibility for getting yourself to and from work on time even though you don't have your car. You learn patience and a few other adaptive skills. Then you either get your car back or the insurance company replaces it, and you carry on as usual.

In taking responsibility for the same thing not happening in the future, there are a few options. An effective car alarm, a steering-wheel lock or a lock-up garage would all help, though nothing is guaranteed if a thief *really* wants the car.

If, however, you had left the car unlocked, with the keys in it, *and* you didn't have comprehensive car insurance, that would be both your fault and your responsibility, and the lesson would be painfully expensive.

I asked Solange to relate this analogy to her state of health. She worked out that having inherited the genetic make-up that predisposed her to her disease was not her fault. But it was her responsibility to herself to eat healthily, rest, exercise, to keep herself as well and happy as she could, and to take medication and supplements if necessary.

Solange realised that early abusive relationships had ruined her health and her morale to the point that she got sick. She had been in Victim for some time. She had been unaware of the consequences of identifying with powerlessness that had unconsciously allowed the disease to start. Solange was learning how to be herself instead of defaulting into Victim, so it would never happen again if she could help it. She began to realise that her present health problems were the result of what her Victim Character had been thinking and feeling years before, and that taking responsibility for a healthy future meant changing her thinking now, especially in not blaming herself. She acknowledged that her health was not necessarily going to improve overnight, just because she was changing her thinking to be kinder to herself now.

She had become so angry at the practitioner because as Victim she had secretly believed she *was* attracting all her bad luck and ill health. When the remedy had failed, she had gone back into the hopelessness of Victim, and it was as Victim that she had gone into her appointment. The practitioner, who felt he had failed her, had then flipped into Persecutor.

By the end of the session Solange did not feel guilty for causing her illness, nor for the remedy failing. While she no longer blamed the practitioner for his treatment of her, she decided she would look for a better one. She also decided that instead of going into future consultations as a pathetic Victim, she would be calmly matter-of-fact about her symptoms and what she had already done to help herself, so her new practitioner could help her further. She would own her situation. She would take responsibility to use the best resources she could find to become healthy once more.

Attracting what we really want

Once we have eliminated unconscious actions, 'negative' emotions and thoughts that bring unwanted results, once we are certain that the energy we are giving out is not attracting misfortune, we can begin to attract what we really want into our lives.

In terms of tragic events, it's only sometimes that what happens to us is karmically attracted, though it could be *samskarically* attracted—not the same thing. Sometimes it's simply a random occurrence and we happen to be in the way.

The most important thing is not *what* happens, but *how we deal with it*. Sometimes we can fix what has gone wrong. Sometimes we can only change our blaming attitude. When we take responsibility for dealing with the problem in the best way we know how, we are no longer at the mercy of unknown forces, a known enemy, fate or God.

In taking responsibility without blame we can be at peace, even in the midst of tragedy. We can trust the process and trust the Divine energy to provide the gifts we need, be it a painful lesson or pleasant. We can trust our own ability to respond in whatever way is needed. And we can accept that what happens is another opportunity to practise enlightenment.

13

Running a Character out

A Character that is allowed to play itself out will sooner or later disappear—like Tom Hanks' 'running man' in the movie *Forrest Gump,* who literally ran non-stop for three years then suddenly came to a halt, turned and walked back home. Similarly a Party Boy or Girl Character can regularly go clubbing, get routinely wasted every weekend for years, then suddenly see no point to it and stop. Or a Martial Artist Character can religiously train and attend tournaments until he has nothing left to prove.

When our choice of career is driven by the desires and fears of a Character, it can rarely be sustained for very long. A Compulsive Helper may become a nurse, doctor, rescue worker, social worker, teacher or therapist, only to leave the profession feeling disillusioned and disappointed. We lose interest in a career when a Character can no longer achieve its aims or it no longer 'works'. To stay in a career once interest or motivation is lost—say for financial reasons—is to cement ourselves irrevocably in a Character.

Running out the Pleaser

As a young boy, Frank desperately wanted to please his lawyer father, an undemonstrative and competitive high achiever. His father groomed him to follow in his own footsteps. He sent him to an expensive private school and insisted he join the school debating and chess clubs. He supervised Frank's choice of subjects until he matriculated and went to law school. After a year or two as a junior in a prestigious law firm, a position secured by his father's influence, Frank found himself less interested in the practice of law and more in his neglected creative side. He left the firm, broke with his father, then trained as an actor, feeling happier and much more at home. In this case, Frank's Lawyer Character ran out before his Pleaser Character. The latter was locked in by his inability ever to win his father's approval. But when he won approval from his audiences, he was enjoying his craft in a way he had never loved law. Eventually, with a lot of work on himself, Frank later also ran out his other-determined Pleaser Character.

Modern times can actually help free us of our Professional Characters. The rapid expansion of technology means fewer people now remain in one career for their entire working life. Retraining, relocating and reinventing ourselves is becoming more common, with some people following three or more careers in one lifetime.

When we suddenly lose interest in something that has previously consumed us, often it is a Character running itself out.

Why are some Characters run out more easily than others?

Characters with chronic emotions of lower energy such as grief and apathy allow little change and their fixed astral structures are difficult to shift. Victim is far more difficult to run out than most other Characters because of the heaviness of its energy and emotions, its low physical action level, its lack of personal space and its high level of manipulative control. Wimp is another difficult Character to run out, and so are Nothing Works for Me, Nice Person and Wet Blanket. All are low-energy, low-action Characters with very little space.

Other Characters have a higher energy vibration—and the more dynamic they are, the easier they are to run out. A low-energy Character attracts slow and sticky energy, and like quicksand in a swamp it will suck energy from all around, depleting others but unable to use the energy itself. The higher the level of energy and physical action in the Character, the greater the chance that it can be played out until it is no longer compulsive.

We can raise our own energy level by keeping physically active and mixing with others who are interested in and enthusiastic about what they are doing. They are also less likely to be in Character or into Character Games, thus allowing us to drop ours.

When we do not resist a Character and play it out consciously and wholeheartedly—*and it can achieve its aims*—then it will fold much more quickly than if it is continually frustrated in its aims. Resistance to any force only makes that force or energy stronger.

Acting angry

The acting technique called The Method, formulated by Konstantin Stanislavski and developed by Lee Strasberg and others, is based on delving within oneself to find the emotion required for a theatrical role in our personal history. So if intense anger is required, the actors recall a past event in their lives which made them angry, to produce 'authentic' anger. Trouble is, by doing this, it's entirely possible to run out the Angry Character, and it then begins to feel 'inauthentic' to play the emotion. The role is no longer motivated by one's reactive anger. Playing it consciously then can *feel* fake, but is actually cleaner, with less risk of the actor identifying with the role so much that he is drained by it.

Some professional actors of great skill rely not on mining their own *samskaric* events but, having discharged any given unresolved emotion, are able to reproduce these cleanly and purely as required. Directors love these professionals, because they can access genuine emotion at will. They tend to be far less temperamental than an actor who immerses himself in a role, becoming it and living it for the duration of the run of the play or film. Like the expert martial artist who does not use reactive anger in sparring matches and tournaments, the energy is focused and uncontaminated by personal aggression or unresolved issues of the past. On the stage, as in the ring, the result is extraordinarily authentic. It's less exhausting than for a Method actor, who takes some time to 'prepare' as well as let it go at the end of the scene or the play. When an actor is not processing his own pain on stage night after night, it's also far more enjoyable for the audience to watch.

14

From Characters to Roles

Nothing in the world is softer and weaker than water
Nothing is better for dissolving the hard and the strong.
Nothing can take the place of water.
All know that the pliant overcomes the presumptuous,
And the tender overcomes the tenacious.

Lao-Tzu, *The Tao Te Ching*, LXXVIII

The fact that a Character can be run out leads to a solution to the whole
Character charade. A Character is largely defined by its compulsive, unconscious nature. When we 'play' the Character consciously and deliberately,
with as full an awareness as we can muster, it changes. It ceases to be a Character and becomes a Role, in which we can be more present and in control.

Once we are aware of our Characters, turning them into Roles that we
play deliberately is the next step in our evolution. The Conscious Triad is a
basic model for this method.

The Conscious Triad

Remember our 'vicious triangle' from Chapter 10—the Karpman Drama
Triangle, that self-perpetuating and ever-revolving Character Game destructively played out by Victim, Rescuer and Persecutor?

The basic energies motivating these three Characters can also be expressed at a higher vibration, a more effective and capable level, when these Characters consciously shake off their automatic, reactive behaviours and adopt instead a higher-functioning Role. In the Conscious Triad, the sense of justice in a Persecutor enables it to step up to benevolent Leader Role; a Rescuer's empathy enables it to take on the Role of True Helper, while a Victim's receptivity and gentleness assume the more empowered Protégé Role (see diagram).

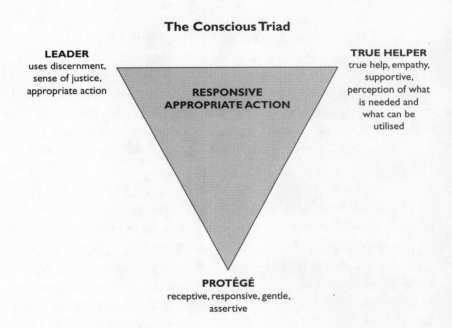

The Conscious Triad

LEADER
uses discernment,
sense of justice,
appropriate action

**RESPONSIVE
APPROPRIATE ACTION**

TRUE HELPER
true help, empathy,
supportive,
perception of what
is needed and
what can be
utilised

PROTÉGÉ
receptive, responsive, gentle,
assertive

From Persecutor to Leader

Look beneath the **Persecutor**'s habitual anger and often its trigger is the sense of something *not being right* coupled with a compelling need to stop whatever it is. Because Persecutor evolves out of Victim, when we are in this Character we often have a feeling of personal injustice and a need to protect a more vulnerable inner part. This means that a *sense of justice* is inherent in our Persecutor, however buried and extreme its expression.

On the higher vibrational level of the Conscious Triad, this energy is still powerful, but rather than destructive and disruptive is creative, dynamic, decisive, protective and benevolent. In the higher frequency the sense of justice is a powerful force for right action and for creative good. By discharging the reactive emotion that feeds our Persecutor Character our behaviour becomes no longer reactive but *responsive*. Rather than automatic or unconscious, our actions become appropriate, consciously discerning and judicious. We take over the Persecutor Character, elevating it into the **Leader** Role.

COMMUNICATING AT A HIGHER LEVEL

Characters often use the accusative 'You . . .', deflecting the spotlight onto the other person. If we realise we are giving our power away by doing this, we can stop for a moment and rephrase using 'I' messages, which more accurately state our viewpoint, feelings and thoughts when attempting to assert ourselves or resolve conflict, and help us take wider responsibility for ourselves.

'I' messages begin with a neutral viewpoint that doesn't blame the other person. 'I feel sad' is a description that doesn't make the other person responsible for our sadness, especially when put into a specific context of time and place, as in 'I feel sad when I hear bad news', or 'I feel frustrated when I ask you a question and you don't respond.' Compare this to the Guilt-Monger's 'You never answer!', 'You always make me feel depressed' or 'You make me so angry', which are unspecific and manipulative and make the other person feel cornered. 'You' messages provoke anger, defensiveness and counter-attack and escalate conflict.

If we are using 'I' messages and someone reacts as though we've accused them of something or are dumping on them, we can instantly see that they are in a Character and using reactive, irresponsible ways of communicating. It's an additional challenge to stay in non-reactive communication ourselves when we encounter this, but if we can handle any internal reactivity of our own, not letting it act out in the conversation, we can achieve what seem to be miracles of conflict resolution.

In terms of energy the Leader Role is not *samskaric* but Egoic. It's not based in the reactive emotion of astral energy. The astral energy of a Persecutor swamps or bulldozes others. Their feeling is of being squashed by sheer dominating force of his astral presence. In contrast, the Leader does not impose himself on the energy of others. Egoic energy is soft, expansive and inclusive.

From Rescuer to True Helper

When we are in the **Rescuer** energy, we have at heart the wish to help, and to be the acknowledged agent of that help. To be needed and wanted and loved and appreciated—that is at the core of this Character. Our Rescuer is needy, yet denies that need. We find, or create, Victims that need it more. Energetically, we parasitically feed on the neediness of others and drain their energy. We have no boundaries and will allow ourselves to be drained, then resent those who have taken advantage of our good will.

In contrast, the energy of the **True Helper** does not rush in compulsively to help, but waits until asked. When we are in True Helper we ask what is needed, then assess that for ourselves. We'll discern whether it is appropriate to supply that need, or other needs we can see instead. For example, to supply an alcoholic's request for alcohol is part of the problem, the position of Enabler. In True Helper we determine whether we can actually help, what resources we can draw upon, to what degree or for how long. We'll note how much help the person in need can actually accept and use.

Give a man a fish . . .

Without being defensive or blocking, as True Helper we are assertive about demands on our time and energy, and unlike Susanna the Rescuer in Chapter 10, do not let ourselves be exploited. We have clear boundaries and safeguard those who have none, helping them define their own. Our help will not demean others, nor will it deprive them of dignity. Rather, we seek pragmatically to empower people to the point that our help may no longer be needed.

The saying 'Give a man a fish and feed him for one day; teach him to fish and feed him for life' describes the effective and empowering support of a True Helper. Some of the best charities espouse this philosophy because it uses their limited resources in the best way.

Abundance is about love, increase and joy. Lack is about loss, need and pain. In True Helper the bountiful energy of the Ego gives from fullness without needing to be needed. We can be unconditional in our love and wise and compassionate in our understanding. This includes knowing what the recipient needs to give in return, in order to use the help we offer effectively.

The art of receiving

There is an art to receiving the gift of true help. Partly it entails recognising the *form* of the gift—that it was not what we asked for, but is what we needed. Often it is of far more value than we could ever pay for, though payment of some kind is essential if we are to make use of it. How do we pay for our lives being changed or enriched, for healing that makes us more whole, for knowledge that puts us in charge of our lives? We need to know that we can return this deeper favour, though we can rarely return it in the form in which we have received it, to the one who helped us. If we can graciously accept the deeper gift as the flow of a tide coming towards us, in due time we can return that flow with all the fullness with which it came to us. Our gift to the giver is to use fully what is given.

In the universal scheme of things, true help is returned by helping someone else in need when we are in a position to do so. We gratefully return the favour to the Universe. If we are in desperate need and we ask for help from the Supreme Being, God or the Universe, we may not get what we think we need, but the Universe will supply according to our ability to flow back and our willingness to receive.

From Victim to Protégé

When we are in **Victim** we are ineffectual, passive, needy and stuck in the conviction of 'I can't'. While hating being in Victim, we focus most, if not all, our attention on the limitations and restrictions that prevent us from succeeding at anything we try, even when we're aware we're creating a self-fulfilling prophecy by an attitude of hopelessness. We give our power away to bullies and let ourselves be affected by things we cannot change. Energetically our Victim drains others, unless they are in their Ego. Identifying with weakness, we hate to ask for help and often can't make use of help that's offered. When our Victim does finally ask for help, we will often plead for or demand it, expecting the helper to take over for us. We abdicate responsibility.

While the Victim Character is the one with the most potential power to stop the Persecutor–Rescuer–Victim Triangle, it's the most difficult Character for us to rise above when we find ourselves in it. We need to find what it takes to do the very last thing we feel like doing. We need to want to take responsibility. We need vigilance in identifying our triggers and *samskaras*. We need determination in countering learned helplessness by balancing negative, critical thinking with conscious positivity. Keep reminding yourself of what you have done well in the past. Pick your battles, don't keep fighting where you cannot win—you can't change others or their reactions, but you can change yourself. Focus on what you can admire in yourself: it'll chip away at self-loathing and change it into self-love. If you feel you're not worth all that hard work, that's the Character thinking. You *can* do it. Remember what this is all about—being who you really are without layers of negativity.

The higher potential of the Victim is the **Protégé**: the bright and active student. Without giving responsibility to others, as Protégé we are receptive and accepting, but also assertive. We are not made less by the fact of needing what others can give. We can be proactive while still asking for guidance or help. We can use initiative within a guided setting as a way of gaining more independence and knowledge. We can accept a lower position in a hierarchy without feeling unequal, or of lower status.

In Egoic energy, the Protégé flows spontaneously and is responsive to what is given and what is required of us. We can *appreciate*—which means we can make what we are given even greater. We can have an openness of demeanour and a freedom that invites interaction. It's the gentle, flowing quality of water, limpid in stillness and brightly rushing over rocks and precipices to become part of the great oneness of the sea.

SPACE EXPANSION EXERCISE

Advanced: Ego expansion

Even though we are always 'in' our Egoic body, we are not always aware of it, nor do we operate with its qualities of warmth, joy and light. It takes conscious practice to be truly in the Ego. There is no reactivity, no grasping. Physical aches and pains and emotional wounds fade. There is an enhanced sense of other spiritual beings around and above us, and a definite sense of something vast, eternal and infinitely wise. And yet, we cannot find this through trying or imagining. We find it through stillness, conscious intention and *knowing*.

1. Sitting in meditation with eyes closed, go deep within to find the 'real you'. It may be the warmth, density or glow you are familiar with; it could be a spark or flame or something tiny. Or it could be simply a sense of 'this is me'. You may find this in your heart, your Third Eye, your belly or your solar plexus. There is no right or wrong location. There needs to be a tangible sense of it, however, a sensation you can associate with it.

2. Gently cup this sense of the real you in 'non-physical hands'. Softly holding it, experience its shape, contours, weight, texture and colour from the outside. As you do this, it may begin to expand all on its own: this is good, but don't force it. Allow it to expand in its own time.

3. As it expands, go inside this sense of the real you. Feel what it is like to be in your own presence. Most people feel safe, warm and strong.

4. As you experience this from the inside, it may continue to expand. Simply allow this natural expansion of your presence to fill the 'egg' around your body (your astral body) and then the room where you are.

5. Your Ego presence should feel different to mere space expansion where you are more aware of your environment. There should be a richness, more light perhaps, or joy. In this expanded space, you will feel qualities and aspects of your true Self, such as warmth, humour, curiosity and strength. Being aware of these qualities, allow yourself to bask in them, allow them to 'land' in you. Appreciate them and they will grow. Be aware of how you have changed the energy in the room now that it is filled with the qualities of your Ego. Let yourself remember this feeling and how you allowed the expansion of the real you from deep within so you can come back to it at will.

---

6. Consider some situations in your life where, being aware as you are now of these qualities, things might be different. How would it feel at work, for example, or with family members? How would others be affected by your expanded Ego energy?

---

7. If you are doing this with a friend or others in the room, open your eyes gently. Feel what it's like to be in Egoic energy, sharing the space with another. If you are alone, practise doing this exercise until you feel confident, then try it where there are other people.

---

8. Remember, Egoic energy is non-invasive and doesn't take up space in the same way as your astral body, your 'personal space', does. The space of the Ego is light and free, and most definitely 'present'.

15

Taking over Roles

Whenever we find ourselves pulled to behave in a certain way, taking it over consciously and doing it deliberately as a Role brings it more under our control. We can then choose whether we want to behave that way, or not.

Finding out how a Character originally arose helps to take the compulsive element or 'charge' out of the *samskaras* at its base. To the degree that we have brought consciousness to its purpose, the Character loses some of its motivating power—so we can deliberately run out a Character by turning it into a Role.

Not a Little Girl anymore

Remember Maddie, the independent businesswoman who'd morph into a Little Girl Character with men? To strengthen her Businesswoman Role, she let everyone know she preferred to be called Madeleine—a name she had never been called, but which made her feel strong and resourceful. She altered her business so that for a period it catered exclusively for women, and her staff comprised mostly strong, creative, independent women like herself. She made an agreement with herself that she'd avoid close relationships with men for a year, and kept that agreement. In the meantime she worked on discharging the *samskaras* which triggered disempowered states, by observing and taking over whenever she felt herself becoming reactive. It meant she could be gentle without being a Doormat, and adaptable without being over-accommodating. Part of this process entailed not seeing her father for the same period.

After a year, Madeleine put herself to the test and began dating again. To her delight, she was now attracting men who were more interested in her as an equal, and was not defaulting into the submissive Pleaser, even with the old triggers. Even more amazing was her new relationship with her father. He no longer treated her as a Little Girl, but seemed interested in her business experiences and even asked her advice for a new venture of his own. She found she could speak adult-to-adult with him for the first time in her life. She was dizzy with exhilaration and pride in what she'd managed to change in herself. When, shortly after, she was able to open her business consultancy to men as well as women, Madeleine knew her compulsive Little Girl Character was no more.

A different tune

Cait was a fine young jazz musician just starting to make her mark. She was exceptionally talented as a performer and composer, but whenever she played, her self-conscious Hypercritical Character was convinced the audience was thinking how awful she was. It happened nearly every time she sat down at the piano. The critical voice of her former piano teacher replayed in her mind, telling her how pathetic her playing was, and that she would never make a jazz musician. The imprint of the *samskaric* cluster and the ensuing Character were associated with the piano itself, its sound, and her actual playing. Inevitably, as she filled with self-loathing, her playing was not her best and the audience began to lose interest. Then she would feel justified in thinking she was hopeless. Identifying with this Hopeless Character infected her whole life with anxiety and depression.

To help break down the hold of these Characters, Cait found within herself a Star Performer/Professional Musician Role who could play the double bass and drums and thrived on both the sound and audience enjoyment. Because the *samskara* was mostly connected to the piano it didn't operate as much when Cait played the double bass. Knowing that Characters identify with certain postures, she became more aware of how she was holding herself when she performed. When standing up to play the double bass she found it was easier to move out of her lower-energy Characters into the conscious Role of Professional Musician.

She worked at the same time on her personal space. The self-conscious Hopeless Character had little personal space and the Hypercritical Character was introverted—but the Star Performer could fill the Opera House with her presence. She expands her space from within, reminding herself that she is not her Characters. Through conscious intention she allows a flowing energy to connect herself, the band members and the audience. Through the expansive joy of this experience she has gradually eliminated the holds of the Hypercritical/Hopeless Characters and their astral structures have all but dissolved. The imprint of the *samskara*, however, is still there. Occasionally, the Hypercritical/Hopeless Characters could be stimulated by the sound of a keyboard itself, it's just that Cait no longer lets it resonate because she has raised her energy to a higher frequency. And now she plays with the deep delight of a true musician, not a Character.

We can pick a Role just as an artist chooses a colour from a palette to enhance the overall canvas of our life. By playing the higher register of any Character as a conscious Role first, we make it more permanent. We may need to organise our lives to avoid old triggers for a while, but dealing with reactive people and reactions within ourselves then becomes a matter of using the appropriate Role and the appropriate energy so that the interaction is no longer a power struggle but has the foundations for genuine communication. Though this phase may seem heavy on the need for conscious control, through it we eventually arrive at spontaneity and freedom.

Playing conscious Roles

Since they often come in pairs or trios, if you decide to run your Characters out by playing them consciously, it makes sense, like Madeleine and Cait, to choose to play the more highly functioning one. There are several reasons for this.

The heavy, sticky energy of a disempowered Character makes it almost impossible to be anything but reactive. The stronger Character also has a larger personal space and is more conscious and more aware. Playing a Character deliberately, making it a conscious Role, means we do it differently to how it plays out when it is automatic. When we play something out consciously, the unconscious motivation for it discharges. There is much to be learned from observing this process.

Certainly society does not accept some Roles. Yet there are opportunities to play out some powerful or potentially dangerous Roles through games, dramatic societies and sport—especially if a Character Workshop is not handy.

Running out a Fearful Character

We can run out a Fearful Character by doing precisely what the Character fears. Often when we do this we find that what we were afraid of was a paper tiger—the actual experience is far less of a problem than we imagined. Our Character was conditioned to be afraid, but we are not. What we are consciously playing out is the higher-energy counterphobic Fearless Role. Playing this Role involves finding inner resources to overcome the paralysis of fear and finding solutions to problems that may once have defeated us. It is a process of developing the 'muscle' of the Will so that it really begins to work. In changing ourselves, problems that once plagued us no longer exist.

In addition to developing our Will, because we are actually achieving certain goals, our self-esteem goes up immeasurably. In feeling good about ourselves we no longer need to seek external approval or attention. We can still feel fear—which is necessary to a degree for our survival—but we are able to respond *appropriately* instead of reactively fleeing, fighting or freezing.

The energy of the more active Fearless Character is lighter and more fluid, and its structure can be more easily broken down than its often paralysed Fearful flipside. Then, when one of the pair has been defused, the entire see-saw structure inherent in the flip loses its cohesion and breaks apart. Eventually, only the Self is left.

Running out the Tyrant

One likely arena for running out a Tyrant Character is in a professional or business situation where a person masquerades as The Boss but, as his staff will attest, is really a Tyrant. For such a person to want to run out his

Tyrant in order to become a more enlightened and Benevolent Boss would be unusual, such is the intoxication of power. Nevertheless, it's possible. As feeble as it sounds, running out a Tyrant Character can be done in as low-keyed a manner as organising a small group social event. In taking responsibility for organising a group event, there are many opportunities to run roughshod over group members in an autocratic manner. Those opportunities, of course, are also challenges to act more in the interests of the whole group. We can be aware of the traps and avoid them. If the event is large enough, we can set up safeguards such as team roles and feedback sheets. If it's a regular event the organiser position could be rotated among committee members. Taking over Tyrant deliberately means that we would do it differently, not as the Character would. We might be able to create a Role of Benevolent Dictator or Efficient Organiser instead.

Running out an Angry Character

Angelica's fiery Latin blood often got her into trouble. When she got angry—which was often—it was sudden and cataclysmic. She would be throwing things at people before anyone had a chance to say anything. Her work tantrums were critically disruptive and endangered her job (as well as other people's heads). She described how she would be taken over by the anger and feel it as a rush, but when it was over she felt fine, having got the emotion off her chest. Her workmates, however, were in pieces, and the provoking situation would rarely be resolved.

Angelica's anger management program entailed three simple elements: stepping back when she felt anger erupting, removing herself to a safe place where she could express it without harm, and releasing her anger completely so she felt calm before she returned to where she had been.

Her first 'safe place' to vent anger at work was near a dumpster in the loading dock. The first time she went there she found polystyrene foam boxes next to the dumpster. Angelica ripped into them, jumping on them, kicking them and smashing them with her fists until they were in tiny pieces. After she felt she'd expressed all her current rage, she'd return to the office, where one or two people eyed her warily until she smiled and they relaxed. When there were people in the loading dock, Angelica retreated to an empty stairwell with a polystyrene or cardboard box and destroyed it there. Or, if there were no boxes, she'd simply go to the stairwell and scream silently. Holding on to her rage until she got to her safe place was her first and hardest achievement.

When her anger began to erupt at home, Angelica went into her garage, where she kept a huge wheelie bin. Inside the bin was a sandstone block. Next to the bin was a pile of chipped plates from a local thrift store. Allowing herself the catharsis of smashing plates into the bin was satisfying without the need to clean up or replace all the precious china she'd destroyed over the years. For a time all these methods were as necessary as her daily shower.

Over some months, Angelica also worked on defusing underlying anger issues. She found she no longer needed to silent-scream, punch foam boxes or smash plates every day, but only every few days. Then it was once a week, and then more infrequently, as her 'compost bin' of old, stored anger was gradually released.

Angelica is still fiery, but now her energy is channelled into a Project Manager Role with such enthusiasm that team members are carried along by her momentum. She is unstoppable until a project is finished. She's made the transition from Persecutor to Leader.

Recently she dealt with a burst of anger as she sat at her desk with a provoking client on the phone. Angelica broke three pencils in half, one-handed, one after another, while she maintained the necessary professional cool with the client. She was amazed that three pencils alone sufficed until she had vented all her triggered anger.

Three pencils: $1.50.

Handling a difficult client, keeping the account *and* knowing you've mastered your own reactive anger: priceless.

Anger and chronic fatigue

Chronic Fatigue Syndrome (CFS) is one of those conditions that baffle the medical profession. There are so many underlying causes, from specific allergies that weaken the immune system to systematic poisonings such as mercury toxicity from dental amalgam, to sensitivities to the chemicals that are everywhere in modern life. Symptoms are equally erratic and wide-ranging.

Many people with CFS are also depressed to varying degrees—and understandably, since their energy is so depleted, their immune systems so compromised and the level of physical pain they daily experience is often overwhelming.

In many cases the underlying causes involve suppression of anger from an early age. Perhaps anger was regarded as socially unacceptable. Perhaps there was an aggressive or bullying person in their family environment from infancy so that any expression of their own anger was met with swift and violent retribution. Regardless of causes, *not being able to express their ongoing and present frustration* is a significant element in people with CFS since they have no energy to do so physically. Apart from talking to a therapist, which helps, often the only way possible is to write down their emotions to get them off their chest. The Three-Day Letter process is one which works well in such situations.

THE THREE-DAY LETTER

In this process, the letter is *never meant to be sent or read by any other person.* Pick a time when you will not be disturbed, turn off your phone and set a timer for an hour. On a writing pad, start writing to the person with whom you are angry. Don't censor yourself in any way; don't worry about spelling or grammar. Vent all your annoyances, no matter how petty they may seem, as well as your frustrations and rage. Allow yourself to say what you'd really like to do to them, if you were not a rational, civilised person. When the hour is up, roll the sheets of paper up and place them *where no-one will find them.*

On the next day, preferably at the same time, repeat the process, reading what you have already written out loud to yourself, then add what has percolated up through the previous 24 hours. Do the same the next day, only on this day when you have finished, have a ceremonial burning of all the sheets of paper.

This powerful cathartic process hurts no-one, takes little physical energy and often has extraordinary results in improved relationships and the beginnings of a healthier emotional life. It's perfect for people with CFS or those who cannot, for various reasons, be more physical in venting their anger. The three-day process might well need several repetitions!

The evolution of anger

When the long period of de-suppression comes to an end, when we have expressed and defused much of our reactive anger and discharged the relevant *samskaras*, what once triggered intense rage, sudden anger or even mere annoyance is rendered harmless. We may find that what used to provoke strong reactions may now be viewed with detached amusement or indifference. Unconsciously a Bored or Conservative Character might emerge. Consciously, in this stage, we may create a Leader or Teacher Role for ourselves, or play with Power-Monger or Politician, among others. Let's say this person is at **Stage V**.

In a person who is well into, but not quite at the end of the lengthy process of de-suppressing anger release in therapy, the sudden surge of anger outside of therapy can indicate that something in the environment is wrong, some injustice is occurring that needs to be stopped. This is often on behalf of someone else, and the anger can be used as motivating power towards stopping the injustice. Consciously employing this anger to develop a True Helper Role can be very effective. If it is not accessed with awareness, unconscious Avenger Characters or Compulsive Helpers may emerge. This is **Stage IV**.

In a person still in the beginning stages of work on himself, or in someone with a great deal of suppressed resentment, there is usually a residual level of anger as an undertow to every emotion and thought. This can be so subliminal that the person is unaware of it. It may come in waves which last for a few days to a few weeks and then recede to mere annoyance. It can feed a Bitch or Bastard Character that reacts indiscriminately and defensively like a wounded or frightened animal, or lead a Persecutor to feel justified in punishing a Victim (as with Tessa). In this case anger motivates actions that may be designed to stop a perceived personal attack, but which are rarely effective against the actual cause because its expression is displaced. Inadvertent explosions of rage then act as guilty reinforcement in further repression of anger. Alternatively a client in therapy might decide this is the right time to deal with anger issues that have been suppressed till now. This is **Stage III**.

Stage II is when a person is so disconnected from his anger that he thinks he has none. It begins when a small child is conditioned to suppress natural anger—say as part of the socialising process implemented with varying degrees of force by primary caregivers. ('Shush, sweetie, it's not nice to shout'; 'Stop it. It's not nice to get angry at your brother/sister/friend'; or

'Shut up, kid, or I'll give you something to yell about!') The ultimate result of ongoing repression is powerful fermented anger which is habitually denied, suppressed and unconsciously projected onto those around him. When those others explode in projected anger, he can react as a Victim, outraged that someone would allow himself to offload in such an uncontrolled way. In an extreme or sociopathic personality, he can be so disconnected that he enjoys the anger that he has covertly manipulated in others, feeling aloofly superior. The Characters that belong in this Stage are all toxic. They're manipulative and Nice Characters: Mummy's Boy or Daddy's Little Princess; Covert Aggressive; Bully, Rescuer or Victim, among others.

Stage I is the natural organic anger of an infant who is thwarted or frustrated in what he wants. It's a clean expression of an emotion and usually vocal and brief, without any significance to it, until disapproval is unhelpfully loaded on by primary caregivers. If it's not an actual problem needing adult intervention, an angry toddler in Stage I can be encouraged to pillow-bash *without significance,* and take Time Out until he feels calm. As a result, suppression of anger will not be an issue.

A child can be taught the safe physical release of anger, after which the non-reactive, rational communication of it can become a communication skill towards conflict resolution. It is only when this is actively prevented that the child will act out his anger unconsciously and destructively. Still, a purely Angry Character can emerge from this Stage if too much attention is given to anger *over* the expression of other emotions. Theoretically, it's possible for a Stage I child who is parented intelligently in this way to skip all the neuroses of the suppressive Stages and find himself at Stages IV or V.

Learning to handle power: Stage VI

A person in Stage V of the evolution of anger may see an injustice and yet feel no reactive anger provoking him to stop the injustice—something other than anger must be used as motivation. Remember our original Sanskrit definition of the word *samskara* is 'motivator'. If our *samskaras* are defused to the degree that large parts of the astral body are discharged, it will not be emotional reactions which determine—motivate—our actions.

An injustice is still an injustice, and if it doesn't make a Stage V person angry, how is he to be motivated to try to stop it, if he can? Injustice is an affront, and a keen sense of justice is inherent in evolved beings, or those who have deconstructed and reconstructed themselves (which amounts to the same thing).

Clear rationality and intelligence, empathy, compassion, responsibility and the perception of what would be best for the greatest number are instead what motivate and guide the Leader's actions to prevent or stop injustice if it is at all possible. This is **Stage VI**.

Taming a little monster

Colin and Marie's son Sam had reached the 'terrible twos', shouting no and having destructive tantrums at the slightest excuse. At first, Sam's tantrums were impervious to any adult attempts at verbal intervention. Deciding another approach was needed, Colin quietly got a pillow, sat on the floor and held his squirming son from behind, with the little boy's back against his own chest and the pillow flat in front of Sam. Holding one arm firmly around the child, he directed one thrashing little fist to the pillow instead. Sam didn't get it at first, but then his attention was caught by Marie in front of him. Marie was also sitting on the floor, with a pillow in front of her, miming angry pillow-bashing. Marie was frowning and hitting her pillow, then looking at Sam and smiling, then hitting the pillow again and shouting nonsense-words at it in mock anger. Sam began to copy her, directing all his fury at the pillow. Colin held him safely until he was sure Sam had got it.

After this intervention, all Sam needed when he was angry was the question, 'Is it time to bash the pillow, Sam? Do you want the pillow?' Sam would nod and run to his bedroom to kill the pillow with convincing sound effects. Colin and Marie encouraged Sam to tell them what he had been angry about, after he'd vented onto the pillow. If it was something that could be rectified, it was. If not, they simply talked till Sam accepted the situation. As he grew up, Sam would occasionally come home from school with a purposeful frown on his face. 'I need to kill the pillow, Mum,' he'd say, and disappear into his room for a few moments. Marie would wait till he came out to tell her what had happened to provoke his anger. Colin and Marie included Sam in family discussions, modelling good communication and listening skills and respect. Decisions were reached by agreement, with a high premium on keeping agreements and changing them only by agreement. As he grew older still, Sam's teachers noted his communication and leadership skills, especially in arbitration between angry pupils, his calm self-confidence and his creative problem-solving. At university Sam is active in the Student Union as well as in extracurricular sports and drama. He is taking a double degree, reading political science and law.

The benevolent use of power is something we learn by first mastering ourselves. It is a minefield in which many have lost their way, seduced instead into dictatorship. Taking responsibility is a start. Ruthless elimination of self-delusion is another essential element. Paradoxically, learning leadership qualities starts with learning how to follow directions and be an effective team member. It enables us to know both sides of the power structure, what we can reasonably expect of team members and what styles of communication are most effective to encourage team spirit and co-operation. We also learn, inevitably, what not to do. We are therefore less likely to abuse those we lead in the future.

Aren't I faking it when I'm playing a Role?

Playing any Role involves reaching into a higher part of ourselves which is non-reactive, unconditioned and conscious. It might be a professional Role with delineated codes of behaviour, knowledge and responsibility. It becomes a Role personal to us when we inhabit *our* idea of operating authentically in it. If we have a concept of the higher aspect of any Character or an idea of how to be in that Role, it means it's already within our Ego and therefore a part we can grow into without being false to our Selves.

At the same time, the phrase 'fake it till you make it' implies we *do* know what is required. In this sense, choosing to be conscious and deliberate in our actions is more authentic than a default life of habit and conditioned reactions.

Playing Roles is a great deal more satisfactory than being in Characters. It's closer to the Self because it's action with awareness. When we develop some confidence, a Role can be spontaneous and real in a way that a Character can never be.

When we can play with Roles life becomes fun. We begin to be more effective in life because we can choose the most appropriate Role. Observing our own process means we can be aware of unconscious Games others may be playing and avoid being drawn into them. In addition, there are increasing situations where we feel no need to play a Role—because the perceived

140

threat which created the necessity for a Character is seen as an illusion. We gain confidence through acting from the Will, and this in turn reduces fear and uncertainty. The absolute joy of meeting other people without the camouflaging masks of Characters makes life vibrant and exciting. In letting go of our Characters, the search for our true destiny takes perspective, laying the foundations for our fulfilment.

The Archetype within

Although Characters are not who we really are and are formed through *samskaric* structures, there is often more than just reactive energy fuelling their behaviour patterns and determining their emotional tone. It is possible to play out one's Characters as conscious Roles and find some truth there. It's possible to step back and reconnect with the true purpose beneath, as we saw with the Conscious Triad. If a Nurse Character takes on the profession of nurse, and runs it out, he or she may find in fact that their Archetype is a true Healer. This will only be discovered by playing the Character out to its fullest extent, to see what is left.

By 'Archetype' I am referring not to the Jungian archetypes, but to a blueprint or higher design we may sense is guiding our evolution in a particular direction. In the sense of its being an original mould it is who we are already, though unmanifest. If the Archetype is the blueprint, the Higher Self is the architect, the agent for manifestation of that blueprint. The Ego, or incarnated Spirit, is the energy by which the Higher Self is revealed in our lives. Characters are a pale, distorted reflection in this evolutionary hierarchy.

The seed of the Archetype—our highest potential, the best of what we are capable of—is therefore often contained within our wounded Characters. Generally, the more empowered the Character, the more chance we have of discovering the Archetype within it. Once a Character has been sourced and discharged, and its behaviour taken over in a conscious Role, the restricting shell that obscures the limitless Archetype dissolves.

At the beginning of the work on Characters, however, simple observation is the best way to discover all the attributes of our Characters, not with any significance of good or bad, but sourcing to find out how, why, what, when and who. It is a good idea to differentiate most between reactive patterns that are *not us* first. What is left gives us a clue to who we may be.

16

Music of the Spheres

Through its very resonance, music can have a powerful effect on Characters. Depending on the type of music, it can cement their astral structures or help deconstruct them. Just as in the Old Testament story in which Joshua's trumpets, accompanied by a great shout of the people, caused the wall of Jericho to come tumbling down, sound can break down an astral structure by introducing a different resonance. Cait's double bass did just that.

The energy in a rigid physical structure such as a wall of stone, bricks and mortar vibrates at an extremely slow rate—so slow that we cannot see it moving. Our physical bodies are composed of energy that vibrates at a much faster rate than the wall.

Etheric (life force) energy moves faster still, and is the domain of measurable vibration through which the experience of sound comes to us on a finer level than just through the ears.

The astral layer of thought and emotion is largely the province of light and so moves even faster. Even so, what slows our astral and etheric bodies down are the *samskaric* structures cemented there which disconnect us from the Ego/Higher Self. The faster our energy can vibrate, the freer we are of the imprisoning shells of a charged astral body, and vice versa.

The larynx and the semi-circular canals of our ears make our body itself an instrument which resonates with sound and vibration. It is therefore possible to use pure sound to deconstruct and then reconstruct the astral body in a more harmonious way.

The power of pure sound

If a sound is pure enough, we can use it on astral/etheric structures, much like a laser is used to cut through physical matter. A 'pure' sound—for example one note bowed on a violin, or the reverberating toll of a bell—can often help shake loose the astral structure of a *samskara*. This can be disturbing. It takes awareness and power of the Will to remain still, let the sound flow over us, deconstructing the *samskara* and the Characters which feed on it without our needing to *do* anything.

Some people experience profound discomfort at the sound of temple bells—particularly Tibetan singing bowls. These sacred instruments create sound when struck by a felt-tipped beater or stroked smoothly in a continuous movement around the outside of the rim with a wooden mallet. The sound is an unearthly humming, a throbbing pulse of overtones and undertones. It reverberates in a concentric wave formation to the walls and back again, creating harmonics through resonance. The bowls are traditionally made of seven different metals, including an ore found in asteroids.

The discomfort some people experience on hearing these sounds is a result of some of their astral and etheric structures being disintegrated around them. The structures are too coarse a frequency to remain intact with the penetrating, high, fine vibration of the bowls, and they simply fall away. The person's rigidified energy, with which he has unconsciously armoured himself, is no longer as dense and so he feels vaguely threatened and unsafe. At this point he usually moves away from the sound as rapidly as possible, and restructures the armoured layer once more with reactive energies 'borrowed' from those around him until he feels comfortable once more.

When a person has begun working on themselves energetically, the deconstructing action of the fine vibration of pure sound on *samskaras* and Characters can be a tremendous boon and a short-cut to freeing them of rigid patterns. Far from being an uncomfortable experience, the harmonies suspend thought. There is nothing but sound, and it's blissfully enjoyable. Tibetan singing bowls are often used for meditation and healing for this reason.

What is 'pure' sound? Try listening to a selection of temple bells, singing bowls, chimes and vocal harmonics, as well as different single instruments from violin to didgeridoo. Then listen to singing voices and see if you can hear reactive emotion being expressed either in the instrument, the voice, or the way the instrument is played. How do they make you feel?

It's a tricky distinction. Are our *samskaras* being triggered, or is it reactive emotion in the singer? Is the emotion melodramatic or does it feel 'true'? Does the experience clearly change the way we feel? Is that change to more clarity, or to more confusion, intensity or heavy emotion? Sometimes we only find out by allowing the sound to wash over us. Generally, a 'pure' sound has first an intensifying and then a clarifying effect, while a sound coming from reactive emotion compounds confusion and takes us deeper into our wounds, our *samskaras*. When we are more used to living in our *samskaras* than in our Ego, this can feel familiar and comfortable while painful at the same time.

Cry me a river . . .

Most people have a favourite piece of music that they listen to when they are in a Sad or Depressed Character. In some cases the music is designed to reassure them that they are not alone in their misery. Others use music to lift them out of a blue mood.

What do you listen to when you feel depressed? Is popular music your refuge? Or are you into classical? Do you listen to one or the other only when you're in a certain mood?

It's intriguing to discover what kind of music your Characters prefer and what kind they dislike. While a lot depends, in terms of personal preference, on our education in particular forms and styles of music, it's often a Character's rigidity which rejects one style over another. Often a whole culture or subculture also accompanies a preferred style of music.

No-one has ever been able to prove that listening to music of any kind has caused a person to commit suicide. However, it's frequently the case that an already disturbed, suicidal individual chooses a form of music which echoes their feelings of isolation, anger and depression. In such cases, it is often a Character choosing what to listen to.

Hitting the right note

Sonja had always been a member of a choir and was proud of her deep alto/contralto voice and the volume she was able to project when singing. She scorned the soprano voices in her choir. Her whole musical appreciation was tuned to a lower pitch.

When she began working on herself and her Characters, Sonja realised that an important part of her was underdeveloped and she'd always avoided it. As a small child she'd formed a Tomboy Character, fierce, combative and self-reliant, as a result of childhood bullying and distant, restrictive parenting that favoured her brother. She scorned dresses—especially pastel-coloured, frilly or lacy ones—and habitually wore untailored men's trousers and shirts. She preferred plain designs in dark blues or browns to ornate decoration in everything from her clothes and hair to her furnishings and car.

Her Tomboy Character regarded anything feminine as weak, manipulative, fake and faintly nauseating. This extended to her sexuality, where Sonja was unable to enjoy softness. She preferred to be the initiator, taking the dominant part in any sexual relationship, wanting only to be 'equal to any man'. She thought she must be bisexual or gay, and had a number of lesbian relationships, though nothing lasting or of great depth. The women she paired with called themselves Radical Lesbian Feminist Separatists, dressing themselves like macho men in camouflage combat fatigues and crewcuts—exactly what they were resisting. Nevertheless, it was through an intense lesbian encounter that she first allowed herself to be seduced. Through it she realised the benefits of receiving tenderness in love-making, and what she might be missing.

Through working on herself, particularly through persistent practices of 'being in the belly' alternating with 'being in the heart', Sonja began to experience the sweet natural sensuality of her body. She began to be more comfortable with femininity. She bought some elegant, form-fitting dresses and sexy underwear. She had her hair done in a chic style and had some lessons in make-up. She never found a flipside to her Tomboy Character in terms of a powerful feminine figure—only a Submissive Character, unassertive, powerless and mute, which she hated with a passion. Sonja decided to explore the Archetypal Venus she suspected was hidden somewhere deep within her.

Sonja's explorations into femininity had unexpected results in the choir. She found her ear was becoming more tuned to the sopranos' descant, and that when she practised at home, her vocal range seemed to be extending to a higher pitch, with a confident volume, than she had ever been able to achieve before. To her amazement, she discovered her new singing voice has a strong four-octave range, whereas before she'd been strong only in one and a half octaves.

Sonja believes that singing as a mezzo-soprano has dislodged and discharged more of her *samskaras* than any other single factor. She has developed a new softness and is most definitely sexier. Her sexuality has deepened and expanded in that she can now receive loving as well as give it. She believes her past liaisons were more a result of an aversion to her Submissive Character with men rather than a love of women. That too has deepened and her current sex life enjoys more spontaneous flow. Also unexpectedly, opening up her new vocal range has meant she is less critical of the world around her. She appreciates more, and is more open in general. She laughs a great deal and is more present in the moment. Sonja now sees her Tomboy Character as a sad, limited, controlling mask.

Singing the True Self

Clara was always late. Her friends were used to picking her up whenever they were to meet somewhere. She would usually have no money for a cab, have no clue about bus timetables or only the vaguest idea of where the rendezvous was or how to get there. Clara had no boundaries at all. Time, money, friendship and possessions were, for her, temporary commodities that had no set ownership. She spent money when she had it with no thought for tomorrow, and would often be offended if someone asked her to leave after outstaying her welcome, or pay for something she was using. Her indignation rarely lasted long. When situations perplexed her she simply moved on, as unconcerned and blithe as a fast-rushing river between banks of tumbled rock.

On the other hand, Clara had the voice of an angel. As a jazz singer she was much sought after, and rarely had problems getting gigs—at least until venue managers came to realise that she would turn up late or not at all, and would sing short sets with long breaks in between, during which she would chat unconcernedly to her friends and patrons, oblivious of the time. She was always surprised when venues cancelled further bookings, or when musicians whom she had engaged to play with her got fed up with not being paid for months, or not being paid at all.

Yet audiences were captivated and her friends loved her. The general consensus was that she was 'impossible but lovely', and people made allowances for her failings and eccentricities, which meant she had less need to change or correct herself.

A bridge to vast spaces

On request, Clara brought a tape of her singing to a Character workshop, where everyone listened, eyes closed and in awe at the purity of her wordless, open-throated vocalese.

Profoundly moved by their response, Clara said that the only time she felt she was truly herself was when she was singing. She felt a connection pulling her vertically to a vast space of blissful spiritual presence, and her voice was somehow a bridge to that space. Her audience felt it in themselves as well.

Clara felt she had a Sleepwalker Character: automatic, unconscious and unfocused. She knew she needed to take over her life in a conscious way, rather than continue just drifting along. But first she needed to master aspects of the physical universe which so befuddled her. Creating structure in her life such as timetables and schedules, planning her day, setting goals, completing tasks and keeping agreements were essential elements in this process of incarnating. Differentiation was her most difficult task: differentiating herself-in-a-body and in her Self instead of merging energetically with everyone she met, taking on their emotions, too. Owning her Characters, her reactions and her emotions was also part of the journey.

Clara got together with other outstanding musicians to make her first CD. She continued her daily meditation and worked on getting things done, effectively and on time. It was a change from dreams which had remained elusive as butterflies for most of her life.

FINDING YOUR 'SOUL NOTE'

Exercise # 1

For this exercise you will need access to a musical instrument such as a piano, or an obliging friend to play the violin for you. Failing that, the

---

voice itself can be your musical instrument (in which case simply sing 'ah' or 'ee' going up the octave, starting anywhere). You might wish to record this whole exploration.

Begin sitting upright on the floor, or a stool if using the piano. Close your eyes and observe your breathing until it is regular and relaxed. Then begin to change your breathing slightly by causing a slight friction on the larynx with the breath. Keep the throat friction going for a few minutes.

Then start the 'ah' or 'ee', going up the octave from middle C, one note at a time. Close your eyes once more and feel the effect of each note on your body, your emotions and thoughts. Record your impressions with each one. Some notes may make you feel the sensation of being in a large open space, while others may give the impression of earth, solid and dense. Still others may evoke the impression of fire or colours, while some may feel liquid. Some notes more than others may evoke an emotional response in you. If there is no marked reaction, do the friction breathing again and try a lower or a higher octave.

Usually we can find a single note which resonates so that it feels as though it expresses one or more *samskaras*. It will be more or less uncomfortable or disturbing. Feeling the effect of this note is bringing into the conscious mind what was previously unconscious. If you are on a piano, remember which note this is. I'll call it the 'reactive note'. Sing it in a vowel sound, experimenting with 'ah', 'ee' and 'oo' to see which expresses the emotion best for you.

Now listen for the note which reminds you of something vast, or inspiring or wonderful. It will be the note which lifts you out of yourself and perhaps gives you a sense of eternity. This note is your 'soul note'.

When this note is played together and held down with the 'reactive note', it has the remarkable effect of dissolving reactive structures. If you are using your voice only, simply go from one to the other, holding the 'soul note' longer and finishing with that in an 'ah' sound. Try the following sequence.

Begin with friction breathing.

Play the 'reactive note' and hold it down, singing 'ah' or another vowel sound.

Let the note go and sit silently with your eyes closed for a moment, listening to the silent, echoing sound-after-the-sound and feeling the effect on the body of energy (the astral and etheric bodies).

Play the 'soul note', hold it down, singing it. Then sit silently feeling the effect.

Play both notes together, or sing the 'soul note'. Do this three times, each time listening to the silent echo and noting the effect on the body of energy.

Following this, if you are musical, it would be interesting to find out which key the favourite melodies and pieces of music of your Characters were written in, and if in fact *your* favourite music is in the key of your 'soul note'.

Interestingly, the key most often picked as inspirational is D Major, traditionally known as the 'key of glory'. It's the key of many trumpet pieces and, among other classical compositions, the key of the Hallelujah chorus from Handel's *Messiah*, Brahms' *Violin Concerto*, Elgar's *Pomp and Circumstance* and Pachelbel's *Canon*. It is also the preferred key for most pop and rock songs. Listen and see if it's the same 'glorious sound' for you.

Exercise #2

A slightly different approach with the 'soul note' is to combine the emotion of the *samskara* with the 'soul note'. The procedure in this case is to sit gently 'holding' the emotion or the charged thought of the *samskara* while playing or singing the 'soul note'. This technique can be effective in helping to discharge a *samskara,* leaving a feeling of lightness.

17

Speeding up evolution

Personal growth doesn't just happen. We need to learn actively from our mistakes.

One of the benefits of doing regular transformational inner work and converting Characters to Roles is that our evolution speeds up and our life direction becomes clearer.

This is often first seen in that soon after beginning to work on ourselves we find new interests. We may not notice until old friends begin to drop away—not without some pain and regret—while new ones take some time to appear. With our old friends our once-shared values and interests seem to be diverging, our aims and goals no longer match. A typical pattern is that as we are changing, we gradually attract different friends. We change our relationships and our jobs and perhaps move house.

All this happens because we discover that the reasons we were relating to certain people, or lived a certain way, were generally dictated by how we saw ourselves according to how we were conditioned—*samskarically*—and therefore not really our true choices at all. Our Characters chose other Characters as friends. Our Characters chose our lifestyle.

When we decide to take over our own lives, true friendship and not Characters are needed. But this doesn't occur overnight.

Traps for the unwary

The path is not without its frustrations. Character work is intentionally destabilising. As soon as we move out of, say, Victim, we notice how much our friends, family and workmates are being Victims. It makes us furious. Because we are *so* not Victim anymore, our anger at how we allowed ourselves to be Victim for so long is projected onto others.

Once we find ourselves in this trap—marked by an undercurrent of impatience and self-righteous anger in every interaction—the next trap is the false sense of superiority that wants to act as Rescuer. We *know* what our friends should do and be. It's difficult to refrain from offering unsolicited advice and help—which simply keeps the other person in the Victim trap. It takes a while before we can let go of our projections and allow others to have their process at their own speed.

The changes mirror our steady progression towards our true Self. It is necessarily a chaotic phase. In all attempts to create order we must first create disorder, as anyone who has cleaned out their garage knows. While chaos can be exciting, like a roller-coaster, it can also be frightening. It's essential that something remains stable in our lives to reassure us that we are not going crazy and to allow a steady forward momentum without panic.

This one stable factor may be that we know for sure we are neither our emotions nor our thoughts. We are not our bodies, our *samskaras*, our Characters or Roles. All of these things fluctuate through time and space: we feel their effect and move on. We ourselves—our true Selves—are a constant and eternal consciousness. We have a limitless capacity just to be, and to be whomever we wish. It is this which speaks to us with the 'still small voice' of Truth and which leads us towards our Archetypes by illuminating what is false in our lives.

If we can hold on to this—even if at first we just glimpse it—no amount of rapid change in our lives can daunt us, though we may feel giddy at times.

Samskaras shout loudly, our bodies can scream, our thoughts distract and emotions wound us—how to find the 'still small voice'?

In the stillness of meditation or in deep transpersonal inner work. Any *regularly practised* technique which develops reflective awareness will work for the true seeker.

Our triune brain

In the Role phase of the work on ourselves, it helps to realise that there are aids in our neuroanatomy to gaining more control over automatic reactions. Once again, it's in increasing our awareness of what influences our emotions and reactions—this time in knowing some basic workings of the human brain. Three main areas of our brain are of interest when we are concerned with Character behaviour. Essentially we have three brains in one and though they interact, and communicate with each other via one-way neural pathways, each has a specific way of functioning.

Two-thirds of our brain are a legacy of our animal forebears. The most primitive part of our brain is in the brain stem at the top of our spine. The reptilian 'R Complex' deals with basic vital functions: the hunger impulse, repetitive functions such as breathing, temperature regulation and fight-or-flight, fear/aggression reflexes. Most of our fear reactions come from this reptilian part of the brain and are instinctual—that is, not dependent on rationality. Thanks to the self-preservation function of our central nervous system of which the reptilian brain is a part, any sudden shock automatically pours adrenaline into our system to prepare for immediate action—fight or flight as required. The physical symptoms of fear can be extreme, including shakiness, dry mouth and loss of control of bodily functions or motor coordination. It is in the etheric or life-force body that we feel these effects. This reptilian part of the brain is involved in any Fearful Character and in more complicated disorders such as Obsessive Compulsive Disorder (OCD), Post Traumatic Stress Disorder (PTSD), and anxiety and panic disorders.

The mammalian brain circles the R Complex and is called the limbic system. The functions of this brain, which we feel in the astral body, are to do with memory, emotions and mood, pleasure and pain. It enables the protection and nursing of young and the impulse to playfulness. It deals with associations with past traumas—and equates events in present time with similar ones in the past, as a survival function.

For example, a gazelle drinking from a water hole is attacked by a leopard. The gazelle immediately flees to safety (fight-or-flight reflex—reptilian brain), but not before the leopard's claws have scored deep wounds on her back. Thereafter, in addition to instinctual caution, every water hole, river or lake is associated in the gazelle's brain with danger, whether or not there is a hidden leopard. The mammalian brain in the gazelle associates all water with peril. In us too, such instant equations arise from the amygdala in the limbic system. It is a learned reflex, but becomes so automatic as to be almost instinctual. The amygdala is Emotional Fear Central, feeds the astral body, and is therefore a breeding ground for Characters.

Our third and most advanced brain is the 'human' brain, the cerebral cortex. It is the largest part and surrounds the other two with the folds and wrinkled aspect with which we are familiar. The cortex has as its functions vision, sensation, orientation, recognition and perception of stimuli, and muscle control. In addition, there is the ability for abstract thought, problem-solving, putting ideas into words and speech, creating memory, and the retention of names. This brain is capable of logic and differential rationality.

Studies in neuroanatomy have shown that even though the cerebral cortex is more evolved than the mammalian and reptilian brains, the one-way neural pathways from Emotional Fear Central in the amygdala to the rational neocortex are far stronger than those going the other way. In other words, instinctual fear reactions, along with their emotional component, can dominate the individual before the rational brain can sort out whether the fear is warranted in the immediate situation, or whether it is just a trigger to a past event: an association. As well, instinctual fear reactions can override rationality, even when we *know* fear is irrational.

The rationality of our human brain, however, is where the higher consciousness of the Ego can come into play. We can calm ourselves down. It takes practice, but the neural pathways from the neocortex back to the amygdala can become strong and habitual, too. Control over our fear, reasonable or not, is possible, as many with panic and anxiety disorders have found.

It means that if we approached the water hole at which our gazelle was attacked, we could assess the danger potential with the advantage of our human brain. While still aware of hammering heart and a dry mouth (reptilian brain), and fear of being shredded by powerful feline claws and teeth as we've seen on the National Geographic Channel (mammalian brain), we can remain consciously in control. Are there rocks or other cover for predators? Are there tracks or spoor of big cats? Can we smell the pungent, feline smell of leopard or lion? Is *what is happening now* the same as *what happened before*?

We have the ability to be conscious of our fear and judge where—what part of the brain—it comes from. In any fear reaction there's a primitive reptilian brain reflex to fight or flight, which causes physical symptoms of increased heart rate etc. There's the emotional component of fear from the amygdala. This might override the fight-or-flight reflex with a freeze alternative, in a case where the brain cannot ascertain the relative survival potential of either fight or flight over the other. Our human brain is capable of discerning whether we need to be afraid or not. However, it still might not be able to assess what might be the best course of action in a genuine situation of terror.

Along with OCD and Anxiety Disorders, a Fearful Character evolves because sudden awareness caused by fright is often alarming and sometimes painful, especially if we can't breathe due to muscle spasms constricting the chest and lungs. There is often an overlaid emotional reaction to the physical symptoms of fear that is more to do with psychological (*samskaric*) significance than with the emotion already evoked in the amygdala. The psychological significance might entail fear of the fear symptoms themselves, or disgust at what we might consider to be weakness.

Quite apart from the fear response of instant alertness, consciousness itself is startling and unsettling. And while we can't eliminate the instinctive fear reactions of the reptilian brain and the amygdala, we *can* reactively suppress our human consciousness to a degree.

When it comes to being aware of ourselves, the consequences of our actions, and what exactly we are doing in our lives, we would often rather retreat into unconsciousness with its lack of thought or cognition. Abdicating awareness comes hand in hand with instinctual fear and habitual anxiety, which reinforce the emotional fear equations leading to our avoiding awareness, in a self-perpetuating system. In other words, it's like living in our *samskaras*. At the same time, it's the evolution of the reasoning human brain which makes this so unpleasant, because the reaction is so atavistic. The human brain is designed for more mastery, taking note of older survival mechanisms, using them where appropriate, and overriding them where needed. Our Egoic consciousness fights to make us more conscious, despite our resistance. Characters exist in this uneasy no-man's land between our primitive reactions and our unwillingness to utilise our human brain effectively, where we ignore our Higher Ego. When we consciously take on a Role, we begin to fulfil our evolutionary potential.

Freeing up energy

It's a landmark step when we have let go our illusions enough for our energy to speed up. By this I mean that we are able to get over emotional upsets more quickly and forgive our mistakes more easily. This in turn means that we can move more quickly, think better and faster. We can achieve more in a shorter time. We become more intelligent as attention that was tied up in suppressing past wounds is released, now free to use on the present. We can see things coming and have time to deal with them before they become a problem or a crisis. Old habits of sentimentality, holding on uselessly to the past or worrying futilely about the future, can still hold us back if we let them.

It's the time of choosing priorities: the present and future, or the past?

It's axiomatic that busy, successful people get more done. They plan, prioritise, they schedule in work, rest and recreation and regularly incorporate new learning on any subject in which they have an interest. They are enthusiastic and effective, and don't waste time on anything they cannot change. They take on responsibilities with confidence. They keep agreements, changing them only by agreement. They're reliable and trustworthy. They're motivated by exhilaration and interest, not by reactive emotion.

On the way to this desirable state, our energy raises to new levels, at first incrementally, so we can achieve more in less time. Meeting the challenges that come our way at this time means we gear ourselves up to a higher stage of our personal evolution. We can respond to situations which we previously had no time for, or simply ignored. We can and *should* take more responsibility, since more of our life is under our control, and we can be effective in whatever we choose to do. Problems become interesting challenges instead of trivial or avoidable crises.

Keeping in the present

Some people are good at starting things, but not so good at maintaining or finishing them. Others can brilliantly maintain and improve what others have started, but baulk at initiating or ending. Still others can end things with no qualms.

Few can do all three without some difficulty, and this more often applies to ending things. We shrink from ending a relationship, even when it's no good for either party. Endings are like a death and we grieve. We hesitate before leaving a less-than-satisfying job. We leave loose ends and, in the same energy, carelessly leave our belongings behind or forget where we put things. It's an indication of being out of the present and having poor boundaries, which means our energy leaks.

One of the things we need to change consciously in this phase is to complete unfinished actions, particularly if we are in the habit of leaving things half done or not properly ended. If you come across dirty cups and plates in a sink at work, are you more likely to wash up someone else's unfinished cycle, or dump more dirty cups in the sink in disgust?

Anything left unfinished, whether ours or someone else's, drains our energy and drags us back to the past—even if only in an angry reaction. We tend to add to mess in this way. If an action is completed, however, we can move on cleanly to the next action without any of our attention leaking to other areas.

Finishing what we begin

In ancient Hinduism, this wisdom is illustrated in what is called the three *gunas*: the three qualities, attitudes or states of being in human life. They also apply to cycles of action.

The first is *rajas*, which is the initiating, dynamic energy of creating or overcoming—goal-oriented and proactive, it is often driven by desire. The second is *satva*, which is peace, clarity, wisdom, fulfilment and unattachment—the energy of becoming. The third is *tamas*, which is sloth, inertia and unconscious ignorance—the energy of undoing and death.

Each of these states manifests in different degrees in human nature—indeed, we can spend our entire lives in Characters that belong to any one of the three, most especially to *tamas* and *rajas*.

In action cycles, the three *gunas* illustrate the different phases of creating/beginning (*rajas*), achievement and sustaining (*satva*), and destroying/ending (*tamas*). By knowing how to balance these three attitudes appropriately, we can achieve a great deal in a minimal time frame. It also enables a highly effective life—one of joy, contentment and peace.

The initial phase of any action or project is marked by a particular kind of energy. The enthusiasm, excitement and creative drive of *rajas* is what carries us over initial obstacles and teething problems to our desired goal. Once achieved, there is a middle phase of sustaining or maintenance. This is the energy of *satva*. Success has been reached, and the project will continue as long as we put in enough energy to maintain it.

Then if we wish to bring the job to completion, we do what is necessary to end the project and tie up loose ends. This may entail cleaning up after ourselves and clearing the area for another action. We can consciously use the 'ending' energy of *tamas* for this.

As an example, consider a gardening project at home. You decide to clear an area to put in some new plants. You perhaps consult a gardening magazine, draw up a plan, buy plants. You clear an old bed, dig extensively and prepare the soil for the new plants. All this hard work is done with the enthusiastic joy of *rajas,* and so hardly feels like any effort at all. Once planted, your beautiful new garden bed will need to be watered, weeded and pruned, but mostly it needs simply to be enjoyed. It's the achievement and maintenance stage of *satva* where comparatively little needs to be done, but each thing is a delight. Each time we put prunings, grass clippings and dead leaves into the compost heap, we are utilising *tamas* in the way that allows new cycles. If, however, the garden is neglected, unwatered and unweeded, it will descend into the chaos and inertia of *tamas* and die.

It also happens if you leave the project unfinished. The plants are left in their pots for weeks, the garden bed remains undug. Weeds flourish, the new plants die in their pots from lack of water and space, by which time you have lost your original plan and your enthusiasm. The entropy of the unfinished project attracts more unfinished actions through lethargy. Rubbish accumulates. People leave more things about, out of place. Gone is the joy and drive of *rajas*, and it takes far more energy to overcome the added inertia of *tamas* to resume the project. Buying more plants is tedious instead of joyous. Chaos generates and accumulates more chaos, there is no clear direction and no clear energy in which to proceed.

Exactly the same thing can happen in a business.

Staying in the present is about finishing our actions. If we cannot complete something properly—a job, a relationship, a communication, a mission—our energy is hung up, our attention divided from what is happening now.

Do what you can to end whatever is incomplete. Even an enormous project which can only be completed in stages benefits if each stage is finished before the next begins, or at least if there are separate through-lines to completion that means unproductive chaos is avoided. Don't let your facility for multi-tasking allow some endings to hang. However, if the project has gone too long uncompleted or you cannot finish it for whatever reason, let the past remain in the past, and let it go with no regrets. Only then can we begin something new with the enthusiasm it deserves and that can take it far.

In evolutionary terms, when a person lives a life of *tamas*, it is pre-personal and unconscious, conditioned and reactive, involving no Will. Most dysfunctional and disempowered Characters embody this attitude of lethargy and passivity.

Rajas is the attitude of *overcoming* and striving. Still conditioned, but motivated by desire to achieve improvement, the Will is awakened. Many functional Characters demonstrate this quality. Conscious Roles can also operate here.

Satva embodies the phase of *becoming*. Peaceful and happy, wise and not driven by desire, in *satva* we are content whatever the outcome of any situation. However, it is most definitely not the apathetic inaction of *tamas*. In *satva*, the awakened Will becomes causative intention. It is where Characters are unnecessary or irrelevant and conscious Roles are employed at will. Archetypal aspects are more apparent. It is the final step to *being*.

A Sleeper wakes

Remember Clara, who described herself as a Sleepwalker in the previous chapter? Clara never stayed anywhere for long, unable to commit to anything permanent. She would spend money as soon as she got it, without a thought for commitments such as rent or loans from friends, and seemed incapable of planning or budgeting. Everything—from going to work to starting relationships—was done on the spur of the moment 'if she felt like it'. She was in the unconscious, unmotivated energy of *tamas*.

Clara had never in her life finished anything. Even her sentences meandered and were left hanging, the original thought unclear and incomplete. Anger repelled her, both her own and that of others. She had no boundaries and was fluidly influenced, though briefly, by everything around her until she moved on. She simply ignored reality, preferring her own fey world. From an astrological perspective, Clara demonstrated much of the planet Neptune in her Dreamer Character. People often said she lived on another planet and there seemed little to indicate that she would ever come down to earth.

One foot in the stars, the other in the mire

Clara was frequently affected by the intense emotions of those around her and troubled by a growing anger and unhappiness within herself. The stage of *rajas*—action, driven by emotion and desire—was beginning in her. She began personal and spiritual growth work and in a regression session discovered a past life in India where she had been a prophetess. Much of her present life then began to make sense. In fact it seemed that much of that past Indian life was still carried in her astral structures. It explained her extraordinary ability to play Indian instruments such as the tabla and sitar and her facility in singing *ragas* without formal training. Her favourite food was Indian and she cooked it without recipes as though born to it. Even Clara's lack of interest in the material world made sense.

After the regression experience Clara said she felt as though she had just woken from a dream. She felt the relevance of the memory was to awaken her to a new purpose in this current life and that was to apply her spirituality to her life in a practical way. After all, the Sanskrit root of the word 'Buddha' means 'to awaken'. Developing boundaries and taking responsibility for her life were her new major tasks.

Lost in Lemuria . . .

For some time Clara's process involved hating her Dreamer Character: she felt she had slept through her life in *tamas* and resented time lost. Working with her in this period meant encouraging her to accept her Dreamer Character for its Archetypal qualities of limitlessness, intuitive perception and unconditional love, while also working on the boundaries and responsibility of the more focused and awake person she wanted to be. One of her main exercises was to finish every action before beginning her next one. Another was to think out clearly what she wanted to say before saying it, and to finish her sentences. She found both of these frustrating and difficult, but persisted because she began to see positive results.

Gradually she became more present in time and space. Through discipline and exercising her Will to complete every action, Clara was able to use her creative talents to connect more with her Self instead of using them to escape or disconnect. She can even—if she sets her mind to it—follow a budget! Today it is through meditation and her sublime singing that she experiences the delights of *satva*.

PART III

Emerging from the chrysalis:
Archetypes

Our birth is but a sleep and a forgetting:
The Soul that rises with us, our life's Star,
Hath had elsewhere its setting,
And cometh from afar:
Not in entire forgetfulness,
And not in utter nakedness,
But trailing clouds of glory do we come
From God, who is our home . . .

William Wordsworth (1770–1850)

18

Towards our inner Archetype

It's no secret that our emotions can often blind us. We can be so angry, frightened, upset or sad that we don't think clearly. We don't notice things in the way we usually would. We operate with less control than usual.

Discharging *samskaras* frees attention that was previously tied up in suppressing the past and its unresolved emotions from our consciousness. It means we are better able to moderate and control our emotions in the present. We are less reactive. Our emotional intelligence or EQ goes up, which means we become more aware of our own and others' emotions, more empathic and compassionate. This measurably raises our rational intelligence as well. We become more aware of what is going on around us. We can take in more information and learn better when we are calm.

Our intuition is also increased as we pick up more clues about people and understand them better through the work we've done on ourselves. When our astral body is discharged of *samskaras*, what we sense from others in terms of thoughts and emotions is less likely to be resonating with our own wounds but more clearly their energy, and it becomes far easier to tell the difference. With our attention in the present and an increased connection to spirit, we might also pick up precognitive messages, have premonitory dreams, and be able to pick up energy and information from objects about people who have previously handled or worn them. Our ability to sense and read energy on a subtle level increases and we are able to tune in to others and tune out at will.

It's becoming more common in psychometric testing for companies not only to profile prospective employees' IQ and EQ, but also their SQ. This is spiritual intelligence. It deals with intuition and empathy as well as integrity and ethics. It's about finding solutions to problems that benefit the largest number of people and leave the smallest footprint. It's not solely about the bottom line nor the most expedient solution, and any business with these values is enlightened indeed. In the short term, such enthusiastic employees are more successful and more effective, their customers happier, their shareholders better beneficiaries. They operate on a high level of energy, achieve a great deal, and find high-level, intelligent and creative solutions to complex problems.

Character evolution eventually lands us here. A fulfilled life—our true Destiny, if you like—is about making a difference to the world that no-one else could make. In the process, we can take Roles at will where necessary. No longer bound or determined by reactive emotion, our energy tied up in the past or in worrying about the future, we can be highly functioning, creative individuals, happy in the present, at peace and enjoying a life with meaning. We can find our life's purpose and re-establish a relationship with our spiritual source. These are goals that shape our journey and allow us to find value in the structures of Characters, through *tamas* and *rajas* to *satva* and beyond personality traits to Beingness.

The Tree of Knowledge

In the Western esoteric tradition, in the biblical myth of the Fall, the core of all *samskaras* is the original wound mankind experienced in the separation from God when expelled from Eden. Until that point, we existed at one with our Creator, wholly cared for, all creation at our command. In that blissful Paradise we were unconscious of ourselves as separate from our Creator. As long as we were obedient to His laws, we were safe in that pre-conscious sleep, with no death, no pain, and no struggle to survive.

When Satan tempted Eve and she chose to eat the fruit of the Tree of Knowledge of Good and Evil, she chose a different destiny for all her unborn children. She chose consciousness rather than the bliss of pre-personal sleep. For mankind, however, that disobedience meant we forfeited our immortality, and were cast out of Paradise.

The pain of consciousness

Consciousness came at a terrible price: death, struggle, toil, pain in bringing forth children, and enmity with all of creation. Yet consciousness also brings knowledge that as spirit, we have an eternal heritage and, at the same time, we are spiritual beings incarnated into gross matter, trapped in bodies of beasts with rational brains. It's a painful cognition, at first. Most of us go through at least a period of trying to resist consciousness and its inherent discomforting pain. To remain unconscious we might choose to obliviate through drugs, alcohol and/or the mesmeric, automatic behaviour of our Characters.

Naturally our early *samskaras* can echo this abandonment in more human scenarios: our mother left us, was cold or died. Our father was brutal or absent. Through this, if we wish, we can project onto God all our resentment at our parental suppression and oppression. But perhaps the most obvious clues as to what immense bliss we have lost are the blind ways we seek it, through our frequent lapses into unconscious pre-personality, or our addictions to consciousness-altering drugs, which amounts to the same thing. We are often moths to the flame of our own annihilation.

Pre-personal sleep to transpersonal liberation

Evolution through incarnation means awakening from pre-personal sleep into the personal stage of individuation and differentiation. It feels like standing up, being vertical after we have been lying horizontal. In the personal stage we discover we are alone: we are different, separated, misunderstood and ineffective. The agony of the personal stage is in seeing what needs to change around us and within us, and feeling that we have only ourselves.

From having been beings of light and levity prior to incarnation, this stage is like gravity to a human infant. It keeps us falling down, but in the process of mastering gravity we learn balance. We also learn the virtues and strengths of verticality, with its connections to the Divine, as opposed to the sleepy indulgence of horizontality. Aspiration can pull us through this phase, literally uplifting us.

The transpersonal stage is one of regaining oneness with the Divine and with all creation while still in human incarnation. This is the true liberation. In this stage, the subtle bodies are infused with Ego presence.

We have defused and transformed enough of our astral body to operate non-reactively. Having evolved through incarnation and through the necessary neuroses and illusions of the personal stage to the transpersonal, we manifest our Archetype as unique individuals at one with the Divine. The Archetype becomes a transparent garment through which we shine.

Our duality is our present responsibility, and our task to transcend.

Returning to Oneness

We are most neurotic when we are divided against ourselves. At the same time, duality is expressed abundantly throughout creation: light and dark; the heavens and the earth; male and female; life and death. The ancient duality of good and evil came from the opposition of the most beautiful of angels, Lucifer, to his creator. Duality—or in another word, opposition—is nature's way of effecting growth and change.

As we progress through the personal stage of evolution, Characters are our first means of seeing who we might be. They are both a blessing and a curse. Initially they help us survive. Then, when through habit they have become rigid and control us, they restrict us to the point of suffocation. At that point we need to break out of their imprisoning shells and grow into our Selves. When Characters run out they don't necessarily disappear. It's more that they evolve or devolve into other Characters with a greater or lesser potential for survival, or into Roles which are purpose designed for more than just survival.

The dualism of Characters is shown in their flipsides, and in this dynamic is also a way to stop the cyclic, reactive game. Stepping back to identify and source our Characters is one of the main tasks of the personal stage, while mastering them constitutes the first steps to the transpersonal stage. We are designed to grow and change.

The gift of opposition

All growth needs resistance to become strong. Think of how we use resistance weight-training in the gym, or consider a crocus pushing its way through frozen soil to answer the much greater force of the call of spring.

Any reactive force against which we struggle cannot continue past a certain point; it either defeats us, or we grow strong enough to match and surpass it. Once we have reached that certain point, our strength is no longer for overcoming obstacles, but for becoming who we truly are, just as a crocus blossoms freely under the sun.

Characters arise and develop through challenge, problems, failure and trauma, but what determines the *kind* of Character we develop to survive? What determines the appearance of a Warrior Character, or a Rebel or Persecutor, instead of a Victim or a Rescuer? In the process of becoming, we might discover our Archetype.

If the Archetype is as high as we can evolve while incarnated, Characters are the first intimations of which direction to go. Far from a sanitised or passionless ideal, the Archetype is a fully realised being which is not rigidly contained in any category, but fluidly responds to any situation. It means that we have the potential to manifest aspects of more than one Archetype in one lifetime, just as on a lower level we manifest several reactive Characters. Archetypes such as Teacher, Healer, Warrior and Lover are not mutually exclusive.

The Archetype is a guide to aspiration, a means to gather knowledge and reinforce our essence, and to build particular spiritual structures that express parts of that whole.

We can discover our Archetype through what is left after the fire of the Ego has burned off the dross of a Character. The vastness of our Archetype speaks to us in a heart's desire that refuses to be quenched. It is a desire to reclaim wholeness.

19

Finding your Archetype

We can aim at an Archetype consciously by seeing what gives us most meaning in our lives, and what, through effort and persistence, has rewarded us most. It will be what we love and what we enjoy.

The Creator

If we are already creative, an artist or a performer, it may be that the Creator is our Archetype. The Creator is evident in actors, illusionists, musicians, singers, songwriters, dancers, acrobats, poets, storytellers, artists, writers, photographers, film-makers and designers.

Then there are sound engineers, soundscape artists and other artist-technicians such as graphic designers and computer-graphics designers, who combine technical knowledge with artistic ability.

The difference between the creative efforts of a Creator Character and an Archetypal Creator is huge. Let's look at nature for an example. How is it that creation is filled with so many beautiful things? Whether you believe in a Divine Creator or in Nature herself as the ultimate architect, evolution favours the elegant, the efficient, the successful and the beautiful. And Nature also favours diversity. Where do we find something ugly? A stagnant pond full of putrefying, decaying matter and dying fish. Air choked with fumes. The destruction of a land through war, drought or deforestation.

Regardless of our depredations on this planet, Nature struggles to reassert balance, to fill in where something has been lost, to compensate for imbalance. When diversity is lost, where there is imbalance, there is ugliness. It appears that the basis of beauty in nature is balance within a rich diversity.

When we see art that is ugly, shocking, disturbing or sad, there's no doubt it expresses someone's painful experience and bitter realisation and their wish to communicate that. We as viewers can empathise with what is often part of the human experience, or we can be made aware of, or stimulated to try to right, a wrong. Art of this kind reflects imbalance and lack of success, and though a valid expression, is not uplifting or enjoyable. It's often catharsis as a therapeutic tool, masquerading as art. A Creator Character struggles to express himself, but he is really expressing the imbalance of his own experience. Nevertheless, it's an evolutionary process. If we can touch the Creator Archetype in ourselves it will be something that transcends our struggles, our failures. It will speak from the highest in us to the aspirations in our audience. It will transport, inspire and delight.

In the broad middle ground of the Creator's evolution from Character to Archetype is the instance of the writer's delight when his characters assume their own voices and demand that their story be told, independent of his story outline. A sculptor can *feel* the finished sculpture emerging from marble or wood. An architect can perceive how a landscape *requires* a particular style of building. An intuitive floral arranger or landscape gardener can sense where flowers and plants 'want' to go, relative to each other. A free-form dancer lets the music move her body from within, while an improvisational musician can hear the notes before he plays them. Such effortless channelling is an Archetypal creative process, connecting to something much more universal than our personal expression.

As Characters, the evolution might progress through a zigzagging path of various combinations of Precocious Little Star, Talented Child Artist and Star Performer, and include shadow manifestations such as Liar, Vandalising Graffitist, Fantasist, Satirist and Starving Artist to the polished artistry of the Performer or Creator Archetype.

When the Creator Archetype is manifesting through an artist, writer or performer, the expression is expansive, often breathtakingly beautiful and inspirational. It inspires awe rather than the cheap shock of provocative art. It might not even be the most technically brilliant or polished. However, it connects us to spiritual aspects of our humanity in a way that is not limited to our imbalances. It will reflect an individual vision and expression. And it is definitely awakening.

What if we are creative, but are neither performers nor artistic in the usual way? What if we are creative with our families, relationships, social and sporting groups or team at work? The principle behind the Creator Archetype is the same. It's seen in what is often termed a 'win–win' situation. With all of this, it maintains balance. It fosters harmony and the success that comes from the diversity of free expression, individuality and freedom.

The Healer

The Healer Archetype seeks to end pain, to make whole. If this is our Archetype, we might first experience this subjectively through our own wounds, our own *samskaras* and our own fragmentation. If our first Character is Victim, we might evolve to Rescuer. From there we might evolve to Nurse, Caretaker or Helper.

We might come through this alchemical process to Wounded Healer: the Character which manifests humility, humanity and compassion through its own woundedness. If we can heal our own wounds, make ourselves whole, we can evolve into the Healer Character, helping others in the way we have healed ourselves.

Whereas the Character of Healer seeks to be recognised as the agent of healing and validated for its skill and knowledge, the Role and then the Archetype simply and unobtrusively heals.

The Teacher

If the Teacher or Guru is our Archetype, our path might evolve through a bossy Know-it-all, flipping back and forth to Perpetual Student, who then trains for a profession such as Coach (especially Life Coach), Instructor or Teacher. Apart from any curriculum we are engaged to teach, the Character is compelled to also teach what we need to learn or reinforce in ourselves, while at the same time seeing ourselves as the benevolent and wise Jug filling a lot of Mugs.

Woe to us if our Characters of Guru, Teacher, Political Leader or Cult Leader succumb to our followers' idolatry. Whatever initial benevolence we once had, whatever passion for transcendence or personal or political freedom, we can too easily become the Persecutor, Tyrant or Dictator, intoxicated with our own power, abusing followers and those in our care.

Aiming for the Teacher Archetype is less about instructing than about providing opportunities for lessons, an environment or situation for an individual to learn what he specifically needs. If we can reach the Teacher Archetype we might also inspire a love of knowledge, and beyond that, of wisdom. When asked by a follower to decide for him, the Teacher Archetype declines—beyond providing sufficient guidance—preferring instead the satisfaction of seeing a student make discoveries for himself.

The Teacher or Guru Archetype might also have aspects of the Sage, which will only answer when asked. The Sage's wisdom creates an energising space of clarity and simplicity around him, which seekers can often tangibly feel. It is a space of awakened consciousness which can reinforce a seeker's own wisdom and awakening by resonance.

The Warrior

If we enjoy a good battle, if challenge or opposition stimulates us and we love matching wits or bodily strength against an opponent, we might have a Warrior Archetype. We might evolve through an assortment of Characters, including any combination of Rescuer, Persecutor, Bully, Trouble-shooter, Soldier, Fighter, Social Activist or Policeman. While in these Characters, our grasping ego shows through pride, aggression and force. If we identify completely with the Warrior, times of peace become times of self-destruction. Evolving out of this and reaching for the Archetype involves employing our strength and skill in selfless service. The Warrior Archetype is an unstoppable force in overcoming any obstacle, including those within ourselves.

The Warrior Archetype is free of all distractions of reactive emotion, of his history, his achievements or his status. He has no unconscious habits. He is disciplined and purposeful. He conserves his energy, he observes the habits of his prey and waits patiently as long as it takes for the prey to cross his path. He does not waste energy or attention on anything that is not related to the task at hand. He is in present time and completely focused. Nothing can divert him from his task, yet he is flexible and unpredictable, and cannot be pinned down.

Scientists and researchers in pursuit of truth are also Warriors in the sense of an unstoppable persistence, the slaying of illusions and fallacies, and a compelling curiosity to know and to penetrate the darkness of ignorance with the light of understanding for the betterment of humanity.

The Lover

If we have touched the Lover Archetype, whether male or female, we know what it is to love unconditionally, to accept completely, to have no requirements that our lover be other than what he or she is. We are equal to and have an appreciation, admiration and enjoyment of the Beloved. Both giving and receiving are a gift; the Beloved's enjoyment is as delightful as our own. Communication is unforced and no topic is taboo. Our lover's growth is not required to be in the same path as our own, but is as important. It's not unlike being in love, but without the illusions and disappointments that arise when romance fades. And yet, when we love unconditionally, we can create the magic of being in love, at will.

An infant's love is likewise unconditional. We first learn the conditional, transactional nature of reactive human relationships from dysfunctional family interactions as we grow, and so develop Characters. Though we know how it should be, as a child we adopt manipulative ploys early on because of the family meme, because that is the way our carers and providers relate to each other, and because they might not recognise unconditional love. For us, survival might entail relinquishing the ideal we have within our Selves, with no guarantee that we can recover it.

Our Lover Archetype might be barely glimpsed through an evolution through Characters such as Needy, Flirt, Dependent/Co-dependent, Manipulative Seducer/Seductress, Emotional Game Player and Unrequited Lover to more adult Promiscuous, Cheater and Heart-breaker Characters. Where as Characters we might seek a Lover to complete us, the Archetype's wholeness encompasses and is enhanced by the wholeness of the Beloved, to a love that both fills and contains all universes, for all time. If we can conceive of this, we can aspire to it.

In astrology, the planetary force of Venus represents the sensuous Lover in the charts of both men and women. If we have this planet strongly aspected in our natal chart, in its lower emanation the Venusian influence is indulgent, selfishly hedonistic or grossly sensual and corrupting. On the positive side, Venus' attributes include a profound and sensitive aesthetic appreciation, a joy in giving and receiving pleasure and an ability to communicate and gently persuade—all of which are aspects of the Lover.

The higher aspect of Venus, like the Archetypal Lover, is a divinely connected and transformational love, intoxicating, full and infinite.

The Mother and the Father

We don't have to be parents to aspire to the Mother or Father Archetypes, for they are the blueprints for nurturing, mentoring and protection. We know them, even if we didn't receive them directly from our own parents.

In many mythologies, Mother (Earth/Moon) and Father (Sky/Sun) bear many of the same respective traits. Warmth, caring, fecundity and nourishment in the Mother; authority, the word of law and impartiality in the Father. In astrology the Mother Archetype is linked to the Moon, with her ever-transient emotions, her waxing warmth and waning coldness, her light and darkness, her fluid manic and depressive phases. Father Saturn is a cold and strict law-giver, distant, rigid, miserly and austere. At a higher level, Saturn gives structure, integrity and dependability, while the Moon's gentle fluidity is soothing, nurturing and adaptable.

If we are parents it is not the mythological Mother and Father archetypes which we hope to reach but an intrinsic blueprint to which all parents—at some point—may aspire, and which a Child recognises by the pre-personal bliss the ideal state provides. It's through the Higher Self that we respond appropriately and lovingly to the Child Archetype and not reactively as the Controlling, Permissive or Neglectful Parent Characters.

As parents we sometimes evolve through variations of these Characters in the process of bringing up our children, only to evolve finally to the Archetype with our grandchildren; others of us will unfortunately repeat on our grandchildren the mistakes we made with our children. If as Parent Characters we project our own deficiencies onto our child, she will develop Characters in reaction. These will then project our deficiencies onto other authority figures as she grows, and in adulthood will continue this until, through psychotherapy or spiritual work, she takes over the job of reparenting herself. Only then can the interrupted evolution of her Ego resume. Parenthood is not for the faint-hearted! It is daunting to realise how easily we can fail, and yet each one of us has survived, more or less, our own parents' failures. We need to forgive their failures, and ours, before we can transcend them.

The Child

The Child Archetype evokes a protective and loving impulse in all healthy human beings. It's not restricted to mankind. Mammals of all species behave similarly, even to young of another species, as evidenced when a human child has fallen into a gorilla enclosure at a zoo, only to be safely held by a female gorilla and protected from hostile troop members. Similar instances have occurred when a child is lost in the wild, only to be found years later, having been brought up by wolves, monkeys or even gazelles.

The Child Character cultivates a pseudo-innocence and supposedly charming helplessness to manipulate the adults around him, and to avoid the pressure of expectations with their inevitable disappointments. This child has had parental expectations pressed too strongly upon him. The developing Child Character seeks parental approval and takes on the job of providing parental happiness.

The Child Archetype has genuine unconditional love, a mercurial openness and innocence that melts the hardest of hearts. The total trust of an infant evokes instant love and guardianship. If a child is fortunate enough to have parents that foster this echo of pre-personal bliss, the personal stage will in time proceed and the Ego has the best chance to land and develop.

A fully realised person may access the unbounded freedom of the Child Archetype at will. We can reach it when we are open and unconditional, playful and flowing in present time, when we laugh in pure joy. Sometimes the harmlessness and unconditional love of the Child Archetype can deconstruct others' hardened Characters in a way nothing else can. It's a role known and employed by some enlightened gurus.

The Goddess: Divine or Demon

If we examine Goddess archetypes based on myths relating to Venus, Isis, Astarte, Inanna, Erishkigal and many of their sisters, it's immediately apparent that unlike male or genderless Archetypes (Healer, Teacher), the female archetypes individually represent an overburdened share of the psychopathologies of Characters. It's an interesting fact, perhaps having more to do with paternalistic—not to say misogynistic—traditions of religion, Classicism and psychology, that many female archetypes are demonised. Biblical, apocryphal and other sacred texts have Eve, Lilith, the Black Madonna, the Magdalene, Kali and Green Tara among others who all feature projections of male fear of feminine power. In Greek and Roman mythology, the Fates and Muses are female, as are the Gorgons and Furies. A goddess is rarely a creator, though she is often seen as a meddler in the creations of her male counterpart. How can we relate to these? As Characters, Prima Donna, Queen Bee, Drama Queen, Diva, Fashion Model and TV/Stage/Film Star are all well known. They can be fun as long as they do not take themselves too seriously. We aspire to the higher aspects of the Goddess Archetype as an epitome of female beauty, serenity, grace, benevolence, enlightened sexuality and fertility, evoking adoration and commanding obedience. In her highest form she empowers and transforms her adorers by resonance with her sublime energy.

The Divine Mother variants of the Goddess Archetype (the Virgin Mary, Kwan Yin, the Black Madonna in some versions, and Buddhist White Tara) feature large in compassion, blessings, healing and protection. The Divine Mother has an earthy understanding of both the feminine and masculine psyches and their vicissitudes. She is chaste, if not sexless. Her bosom is for nurturing, not sexual enticement. She is wise beyond ages. She is the Mother of us all. She is Gaia, she is the Earth. She is also Queen of Heaven. She brings spiritual liberation and nirvana.

The shadow archetype of Demon Mother is Lilith, first wife of Adam. Unlike Eve she was created equally out of the dust of the earth. She turned her back on Adam and Eden when required to be submissive to him. Lilith agreed only to be subservient to her Creator and was disillusioned that He would require her to serve her equal. Her furious disappointment with her heavenly Father transformed her into the terrible Mother, devourer of children and killer of pregnant women. She seduces men, then eats them.

She is our own self-devouring and vengeful passion. Other versions of this archetype exist in Erishkigal and Kali. She is the witch and sorceress, dealer in the black arts: vicious, unforgiving, rapacious and cannibalistic.

Lilith has a purer side nevertheless, and has long been hoisted as a feminist icon for her strength and independence of spirit, her lonely integrity, her determination to be subject to no-one and follow none but her own intuitive wisdom.

The Supreme Ruler: King or Queen

As Supreme Ruler the King or Queen is the Archetypal manifestation of the Leader Role. His evolution begins in the least conscious power-based Characters: Bully, Petty Tyrant, Persecutor and the criminal exploitation and self-aggrandisement of Dictator. Higher forms of Benevolent Leader can also arise. Any hierarchy of organisation, business, armed forces or government allows the possibility of the corrupting influence of power, and less often, nobility.

The judicious, strong leadership of the true King or Queen inspires enthusiastic obedience, loyalty and trust and unites followers in one purpose. It is a wise King indeed who sees his responsibility both to his subjects and subordinates and to the greater power of the Divine above him, whose representative he is.

The Clown, the Trickster and the Wise Fool

The Clown or the Fool is an Archetypal figure of fun. As such, he upsets expectations and creates surprise. He represents the Fool in all men and we may all feel superior to him. When we touch this Archetype we are child-like and ingenuous, we win against all expectation, and we are delighted and surprised. The Clown is as superficial as thistledown and as spontaneous and free. He is able to survive tragedies and catastrophes by his very levity. He never realises he is in trouble and is oblivious of warnings. He is mankind clad solely in his self-conceit and the self-delusion of his brilliance, but he is too unaware ever to know this. He relieves us that we are not so foolish, though we are glad his lessons, which he eternally fails to learn, are not ours.

As a Character a Clown can fail tragically to amuse, because the Character is *trying* to be funny. He fails to connect with his audience and may turn to abuse them instead. The Clown, Joker or Stand-up Comedian Character tries, through gross scatological humour and sexual denigration of women—especially mothers-in-law—to project false hilarity and levity to counteract his own depression and powerlessness. There is a subtype of Sad Clown Character which might amuse by being so morose. Through horror movies there is another subtype of Clown With Menace. These are all Performer Characters epitomising obvious facades. In contrast, the Clown Archetype has a transparent simplicity and joy.

The Trickster is another mythological figure, far more aware and manipulative than the innocent Clown. He meddles like Shakespeare's playful Puck with gleeful mischief or the evil intent of Iago's malice. Some Gurus and Spiritual Teachers utilise this Archetype to befuddle their followers into letting go of rigid preconceptions and belief systems. Early twentieth-century mystic George Gurdjieff devised processes of deconstruction which necessarily took sober spiritual seekers way beyond their comfort zone to challenge both conforming identities and inherited morality. He required monogamous couples among his students to engage in an orgy and tee-totallers to get drunk. The Archetype confuses through appearing to be a Character such as Practical Joker, Con-Man or Fraudster, to awaken discernment in the gullible. The Trickster may appear to operate outside the laws of karma. Nevertheless, because of his acute perception he cannot fool himself. This Archetype seeks to enlighten through the catalysts of surprise and disillusionment. As a mode for creating change and increased awareness it is swift and effective, often due to the element of shock.

The Wise Fool is an evolution of the Trickster Archetype, whose shock tactics can have unpredictable consequences. The simple Fool Character, on a flip from Know-it-all or Didactic Teacher/Instructor can also evolve into it. The Wise Fool is something like the character of Lieutenant Columbo in the long-running television series starring Peter Falk. He knows more than he lets on, and trips the unwary and the guilty into revealing more than they wish. In the Archetype the Wise Fool disarms the egotistical and arrogant by simplicity and seeming obtuseness. The aim is to increase awareness by disillusionment—which is always the beginning of enlightenment.

20

An Archetype landing

Do you have the patience to wait
Till your mud settles and the water is clear?
Can you remain unmoving
Till the right action arises by itself?

Lao-Tzu, *The Tao Te Ching*, XV

The Archetype is a translucent garment worn to express individuality in a specific form for the period of our becoming. Not being a stereotype, an Archetype manifests differently from one person to another, starting with Characters and evolving through progressively more truthful definitions of who we are.

As we evolve through Characters and Roles, and if we aspire to the expansiveness of an Archetype, our true Self is a gradually emerging principle which becomes more apparent and more permanent. We can use the early conditioning which informed our Characters and be guided in the direction of an Archetypal emergence, but the Archetype is not a conditioned element, rather a 'landing' of a higher essence which shapes the being as we become our Selves. It is free and limitless. It is part of the eternal spark of consciousness which is our true nature.

From Victim to true Warrior

Stephen is a third *dan* karate instructor who runs his own *dojo*. He is single and paying off the mortgage on an elegant cliff-side house flanked by high walls that keep out prying eyes. His Martial Arts Instructor Character's main philosophy of life was that if you are armed for war you find peace, but he had not found any truth in this, especially as he enjoys fighting. Astrologically, Stephen has a great deal of the planet Mars in his permanent Character.

Stephen meditated occasionally because he felt he should, though he found the practice somewhat puzzling and was not sure what was supposed to *happen*. His main interest was in the fitness and fighting skills of his profession, and in the female students who regularly fell into his arms. The decor of his home contained just enough oriental mystique in its Japanese screens, delicate water-colours and ceremonial samurai swords to intrigue the passing parade of bored young women seeking adventure on his futon. In his home gym, mirrors lined one wall and a collection of swords, knives and other weapons was mounted on another.

Stephen's main priority was the continued success of his *dojo*, both financially and as a magnet for his amorous partners. Mostly in the energy of *rajas*, he taught how to be a single-minded fighting machine and he made a point of never letting anyone else win, ever, in any interaction with him, whether in the *dojo* or out. He believed his Martial Arts Instructor Character was more the Warrior Role, though it was based on his fear and distrust both of others and of himself. The Character let him feel important in a way that he himself did not feel, deep down.

The Warrior is also an Archetype that led Stephen to find ways of dealing with the disempowerment of his Victim Character, which developed through schoolyard bullying and his father's scorn at his slight frame. Stephen's *samskaras* were mostly to do with feeling small and stupid. He often felt betrayed by his mother, who would extract his hesitant confidences and then report them with derision to his father or visiting friends. As an adult, Stephen reacted furiously to any hint that he was being mocked and had once or twice used violence to 'teach people a lesson'. He feared intimacy, and his distrust of women was enormous. He only permitted himself to interact with them in situations where he could exert power over them, usually in a sexual context. His focus was on *overcoming* rather than becoming.

Stephen was already utilising the Role of Martial Arts Instructor when he was asked, as one of a few presenters, to attend a weekend of spiritual practices. In a meditation segment given by another presenter, he unexpectedly reached a level of blissful peace and awareness he had never before experienced, and suddenly much of what he had learned previously in a theoretical way clicked into place. To deepen this extraordinary new experience he joined the meditation school. This was a revolutionary change for him. It would never have been acceptable to the Martial Arts Instructor Character to become a student outside a field in which he was expert. Through the practices, he became aware of the energetic blocks he had placed defensively in his belly to keep people out. After many months working on letting go of fear and defensiveness and on softening his energy in a Venusian way, Stephen's energy is now far more gentle and responsive. Now, for the first time in his life, he has a loving relationship he regards as long term, and his *dojo* has doubled in students. In the *dojo* he now has a meditation teacher giving beginner classes, which he also attends. Paradoxically, he has found his fighting skills have also benefited: he is faster, more unpredictable, and having more playful fun in sparring and teaching. This would have been impossible for his previous Character.

Unlike the Warrior Character, the Warrior Archetype doesn't *need* to fight to prove himself, nor does he need to win every battle in order to win the war. In fact, it may be strategically more advantageous on occasions to retreat in order to win a better position. The true Warrior doesn't resist a stronger force. As in jujitsu or aikido, when pushed, he pulls; when pulled, he pushes and uses circular motion to confound an opponent. He combines his own energy with his sparring partner's in the direction it is already going, to unbalance and down him. The Warrior Archetype is neither predictable nor able to be pinned down. He survives by being flexible and striking only when he can achieve his goal, thereby not wasting his strength. He is far more present and can move fast because he has no attachments and nothing to hold him back, including fear.

And naturally the Warrior Archetype is found in women as well as men.

From Control Freak to Healer

A slim, petite redhead, Tania's face was a pale, calm mask that rarely showed emotion, though her eyes frequently glittered with cynicism. Many people found her a little hard to take. She was most often in her self-styled Bitch Character, in which she displayed no sympathy for anyone with problems. In her job as manager of a medical practice she was extremely efficient and valued because her Control Freak Character could keep the records of seven doctors in order. Her filing systems were precise, but she criticised coldly anyone who disrupted the order she created.

Though she loved her two kids, she was too impatient to have them with her when working her second job, a home-based aromatherapy practice. A perfectionist who was obsessive about cleaning, the Control Freak Character had many Saturnian aspects.

The real reason she worked so hard, keeping her children and everyone else at arm's length, was her fear of being rejected or abandoned. She had worried constantly that her husband would leave until finally, he did. It was only years later in a therapy session that she realised how she had created the growing distrust between them and driven him to find someone more relaxed and loving.

When she was a child she felt she was a nuisance to her mother and irrelevant to her father. Her mother and her grandmother were both obsessive house cleaners and she suffered from their criticism. Little children love to copy mummy and Tania was a naturally orderly child who would pull things out of cupboards and put them back in the neatest of rows. Or she would clean cupboard doors lovingly with a cloth, just as her mother did. However, when her mother saw her doing these things she would stop her, complaining that Tania was making even more work for her.

Once, when Tania was twelve, her mother was resting before a dinner party. Tania thought she would help by cleaning the bathroom. When her mother awoke, Tania proudly told her what she had done, expecting appreciation. Instead, her mother was outraged, saying that she had already cleaned the bathroom and now she would have to do it again, because Tania could never get anything right.

Stung, Tania's Wounded Character decided she hated her parents most in the whole world and one day she would kill herself and then they'd be sorry. In the meantime, she made a decision never to expect anyone to love her or even like her. She decided she would never let anyone get close to her ever again.

In Tania's mind, hate became more powerful than love. Love made her vulnerable. Even though she loathed everything her parents did, they were modelling for her the only powerful adult roles she knew. Consciously she resisted everything about them. Unconsciously she became exactly like them. Years later, coming to realise this in a session, Tania let herself howl with rage and pain. It was the turning point, when she began to allow herself to heal.

Tania's work on herself began to reveal the soft vulnerability of her Defensive flipside. In her interactions with her ex-husband and others, Tania had often projected her uncertainty and self-hatred onto them. She was so afraid that her husband would reject her that she made it happen rather than wait for it to happen. This in itself was a distorted attempt to empower herself, albeit in a self-defeating manner.

In sourcing and defusing her *samskaras*, Tania gradually found she was less reactive with her children and workmates. She finds less reason to act out the Bitch Character. Much of the work she is doing on herself involves consciously finding things to admire in her environment, since what we admire evokes expansiveness and appreciation within us. She works on releasing her fear. She does this in the ISIS process by going into the stillness of the Third Eye. She gently 'holds' the emotions of fear or rejection that are the basis of her Characters, then slowly allows the emotions to expand. Without the resistance she would once have used to push them away, they begin to discharge. With more space the emotions are less concentrated and less reactive, and the Character structures begin to loosen. As well, in the stillness, she has come to recognise the sweetness of her own presence in her heart instead of the cold contraction of fear. By allowing that presence—which is her Ego—to expand in the same way, her energy field densifies to the point where she no longer feels the need to be defensive or to attack others. As well as practising this in daily meditation, she's begun doing this whenever she comes into a challenging situation, and at work it made an extraordinary improvement to office harmony. She began to like herself more and the thought of someone getting close to her became much less terrifying.

Her aromatherapy practice was beginning to lose its challenge, so she decided she would do a postgraduate degree in counselling. She had come a long way from the Defensive/Bitch Character. She was now warm and empathic and an intuitive, responsive listener. She felt more her true Self than she had ever been.

Rediscovering unconditional love

It was Tania's babies who acted subtly on her first to allow her to soften her rigid self-control. In their wholly accepting eyes Tania rediscovered unconditional love. Even if she had not had her own children, she could have done this through a gentle connection with her own inner child, whose innocence and complete love can heal our subsequent wounds.

Tania began to relax and found herself opening parts of her heart she had intentionally closed off as a child, in a cold, critical home. She began to allow herself to be playful. In accepting herself more, she became less judgmental of others. In her aromatherapy practice she found clues to her Healer Archetype, which now informs her counselling practice. She enjoys helping people let go of old limiting beliefs, finding she is sensitive to their needs and adaptable in helping them change in ways they decide are needed.

Tania worked on her relationship with her children, too. They were at kindergarten and primary-school age, stroppy, rebellious and chafing under their mother's formerly hypercritical attitudes. She began by letting them be responsible for the state of their own rooms and refrained from criticising. She would help them make pancakes, managing to grin when sticky little fingers smeared her spotless cupboard doors. She found ways to praise them and this practice has become second nature as she is kinder to herself. They have responded with enthusiasm and are the loving, bright children she herself was prevented from being. Tania recognised all these as significant landmarks in her progress to unconditional self-acceptance and acceptance of others.

She is giving this back to the universe in her counselling practice, helping others to find the same joyous state.

A life rich beyond imagining

Whether we are at the beginning of our journey towards the true Self, near the end or muddling along somewhere in the middle, the key to being who we really are is in living in the present. It's in responding to the intrinsic beauty of this world with an appreciation that resonates in joy. It's in feeling the softness of a rose petal while letting its colour and fragrance fill the secret places in your heart. It's in seeing shafts of light spear down through trees in an autumn landscape, or rejoicing in a puddle of the sun's warmth under wintry skies. It's in the rough texture of stone, the enlivening smell of lemons or coffee, the pure delight in the laughter of children.

When we no longer react to current triggers of past pain but instead respond to what is happening now, our experience becomes rich beyond imagining and we live with joy and awareness. When we are no longer afraid of paper tigers, we can approach life with openness, confident in our creativity to deal with any challenge. When we have faced our fears to do what our heart desires, we can communicate with others in love and acceptance and deep connection. Taking responsibility for our lives is an exhilarating liberation. When we have stood up to our demons and taken back our power from those to whom we gave it, we are free to Be.

Contact websites

www.avrilcarruthers.com
www.clairvision.org
http://in.integralinstitute.org

Bibliography

Allison, R.B. 1995, *Working with the Inner Self Helper During and After Therapy*, Workshop Manual for the 12th Annual Fall Conference of the International Society for the Study of Dissociation, 14 September, Orlando, Florida.

Allison, R.B. & Schwartz, T. 1980, *Minds in Many Pieces: Revealing the Spiritual Side of Multiple Personality Disorder*, Rawson/Wade, New York.

Bloom, H.K. 1995, *The Lucifer Principle: A Scientific Expedition into the Forces of History*, Allen & Unwin, Sydney. (On memes)

Karpman, S. 1968, 'Fairy Tales and Script Drama Analysis', *Transactional Analysis Bulletin*, vol. 7, no. 26, pp. 39–43.

Putnam, F. 1989, *Diagnosis and Treatment of Multiple Personality Disorder*, Guildford, New York.

Schnarch, D. 1991, *Constructing the Sexual Crucible*, W.H. Norton, New York.

——1997, *Passionate Marriage*, W.H. Norton, New York.

——2002, *Resurrecting Sex*, Scribe Publications, Melbourne.

Index